A Soldier of the Seventy-First

A Soldier of the Seventy-First

From De La Plata to the Battle of Waterloo, 1806–1815

By

Joseph Sinclair

Edited and Introduced by Stuart Reid

Frontline Books, London

A Soldier of the Seventy-First: From de la Plata to the Battle of Waterloo,
1806–1815

This edition published in 2010 by Frontline Books, an imprint of Pen &
Sword Books Limited, 47 Church Street, Barnsley, S. Yorkshire, S70 2AS
www.frontline-books.com

*The Journal of a Soldier of the 71st or Glasgow Regiment, Highland Light
Infantry from 1806–1815* appears to have been published in Edinburgh
in 1819, though no copy is extant. It was reissued in 1831 by Constable
(Edinburgh). The most recent version, edited by Christopher Hibbert, was
published in abridged form by Leo Cooper in 1975. This edition is based
upon the full text of the 1831 edition, and includes a new introduction by
Stuart Reid, who also edited the text.

ISBN: 978-1-84832-561-6

For more information on our books, please visit
www.frontline-books.com, email info@frontline-books.com
or write to us at the above address.

Typeset by JCS Publishing Services Ltd, www.jcs-publishing.co.uk

Printed and bound in the UK by CPI Mackays, Chatham ME5 8TD

CONTENTS

For Tom; a book about a namesake

INTRODUCTION

The *Journal of a Soldier of the 71st or Glasgow Regiment, Highland Light Infantry from 1806–1815* was originally published in Edinburgh in 1819. It probably appeared as a part work in one of the many literary magazines of the day since no trace of that initial edition can be found, but it deservedly caught the public imagination and soon went through the first of a succession of book editions.

Latterly publishers have relied upon an abridged version, edited by Christopher Hibbert in 1975, but the present one is based upon the full text of the 1831 edition, published by Constable in Edinburgh.

Other than referring to himself as Thomas, the author has until now been anonymous, although the editor is known to have been a man named John Howell. Although he himself is sometimes carelessly identified as the soldier in question, Howell, born in Edinburgh in 1788, never served with the 71st or with any other regiment for that matter, but was an Edinburgh-based hack writer, publisher and occasional inventor. His known works include *An Essay on the War-Galleys of the Ancients* (1826), *The Life and Adventures of Alexander Selkirk* (1829), *The Life of Alexander Alexander* (1830) and *The Life of John Nichol, the Mariner*. He contributed several stories to John Mackay Wilson's *Tales of the Borders* (1835–40).[1]

9

This present book is, however, undoubtedly his most important, and according to an inscription which he left in a copy of the third edition (now in the possession of the Royal Highland Fusiliers) 'James Todd is the individual I got the greater part of the journal from.'

At first sight that statement seems straightforward enough, for as it turns out there was indeed a man named James Todd serving in the 71st during the Napoleonic Wars. However, there is still a major problem with this easy identification, for Howell then went on to say that: 'When he (Todd) left me I got one Archd. [Archibald] Gavin to fill in any part we had missed and to establish any fact I doubted I had recourse to the testimony of a party of the 71st at the time in Edin.' Clearly therefore it was a composite effort and, as we shall shortly see, the evidence of the 71st muster rolls leaves no doubt whatsoever that the 'Thomas' of the journal who went to South America and Private James Todd are *not* one and the same man. Nevertheless, there is no doubting that their individual stories are authentic, and so we will start at the beginning.

1

THE Writer's parentage and education – Attempts the Stage, and fails – Joins a recruiting party, and sails for the Isle of Wight – Adventure there.

From motives of delicacy, which the narrative will explain, I choose to conceal my name, the knowledge of which can be of little importance to the reader. I pledge myself to write nothing but what came under my own observation, and what I was personally engaged in.

I was born of poor but respectable parents, in Edinburgh, who bestowed upon me an education superior to my rank in life. It was their ambition to educate me for one of the learned professions; my mother wishing me to be a clergyman, my father, to be a writer. They kept from themselves many comforts, that I might appear genteel, and attend the best schools: my brothers and sister did not appear to belong to the same family. My parents had three children, two boys and a girl, besides myself. On me alone was lavished all their care. My brothers, John and William, could read and write, and, at the age of twelve years, were bound apprentices to trades. My sister Jane was made, at home, a servant of all-work, to assist my mother. I alone was a gentleman in a house of poverty.

My father had, for some time, been in a bad state of health, and unable to follow his usual employment. I was unable to earn any thing for our support. In fact, I was a burden upon the family. The only certain income we had was the board of my two brothers, and a weekly allowance from a benefit society, of which my father was a member. The whole sum was five shillings for my brothers, and six from the society, which were soon to be reduced to three, as the time of full sick-money was almost expired.

I do confess (as I intend to conceal nothing) this distressed state of affairs softened not my heart. I became sullen and discontented at the abridgment of my usual comforts; and, unnatural wretch that I was! I vented that spleen upon my already too distressed parents. My former studies were no longer followed, for want of means to appear as I was wont. That innate principle of exertion, that can make a man struggle with, and support him in the greatest difficulties, had been stifled in me by indulgence and indolence. I forsook my former school-fellows, and got acquainted with others, alas! not for the better.

I was now sixteen years of age[1], tall and well made, of a genteel appearance and address. Amongst my new acquaintances, were a few who had formed themselves into a spouting club, where plays were acted to small parties of friends, who were liberal in their encomiums. I was quite bewildered with their praise, and thought of nothing but becoming another Roscius,[2] making a fortune, and acquiring a deathless name. I forsook my classical authors for Shakespeare, and the study of the stage. Thus, notwithstanding the many tears of my mother, and entreaties of my father, I hurried to ruin. I was seldom at home, as my parents constantly remonstrated with me on the folly of my proceedings. This I could not endure: I had been encouraged and assisted by them in all my former whims. All my undertakings were looked upon by them as the doings of a superior genius. To be crossed now, I thought the most unjust and cruel treatment.

I had, through the interference of my new acquaintances, got introduced to the Manager of the Theatre at Edinburgh, who was pleased with my manner and appearance. The day was fixed on which I was to make my trial. I had now attained the summit of my first ambition. I had not the most distant doubt of my success. Universal applause, crowded houses, and wealth, all danced before my imagination. Intoxicated with joy, I went home to my parents. Never shall the agony of their looks be effaced from my memory. My mother's grief was loud and heart-rending, but my father's harrowed up my very soul. It was the look of despair – the expression of his blasted prospects – prospects he had so long looked forward to with hope and joy – hopes, that had supported him in all his toil and privations, crushed in the dust. It was too much; his eyes at length filled with tears, and, raising them to heaven, he only said, or rather groaned, 'God, thy ways are just and wise; thou hast seen it necessary to punish my foolish partiality and pride: but, O God! forgive the instrument of my punishment.' Must I confess, I turned upon my heel, and said, with the most cool indifference, (so much had the indulgence of my former life blunted my feelings towards my parents), 'When I am courted and praised by all, and have made you independent, you will think otherwise of my choice.' 'Never, never,' he replied; 'you bring my gray hairs with sorrow to the grave.' – 'Thomas, Thomas, you will have our deaths to answer for,' was all my mother could say; tears and sobs choked her utterance.

I was immovable in my resolves. The bills were printed, and I had given my word. This was the last time I ever saw them both. The scene has embittered all my former days, and still haunts me in all my hours of thought. Often, like an avenging spirit, it starts up in my most tranquil hours, and deprives me of my peace. Often, in the dead of night, when on duty, a solitary sentinel, has it wrung from my breast a groan of remorse.

Scarce had I left the house, when a sensation of horror at what I had done pierced my heart. I thought the echo of my steps sounded, 'You will have our deaths to answer for!' I started, and turned back to throw myself at the feet of my parents, and implore their forgiveness. Already I was at the door, when I met one of my new acquaintances, who inquired what detained me? I said, 'I must not go; my parents are against my going, and I am resolved to obey them.' He laughed at my weakness, as he called it. I stood unmoved. Then, with an affected scorn, he said I was afraid, conscious I was unable to perform what I had taken upon me. Fired by his taunts, my good resolves vanished and I once more left my parents' door, resolved to follow the bent of my own inclinations.

I went to the Theatre, and prepared for my appearance. The house was crowded to excess. I came upon the stage with a fluttering heart, amidst universal silence. I bowed, and attempted to speak; my lips obeyed the impulse, but my voice had fled. In that moment of bitter agony and shame, my punishment commenced. I trembled; a cold sweat oozed through every pore; my father and mother's words rung in my ears; my senses became confused; hisses began from the audience; I utterly failed. From the confusion of my mind, I could not even comprehend the place in which I stood. To conclude, I shrunk unseen from the Theatre, bewildered, and in a state of despair.

I wandered the whole night. In the morning early, meeting a party of recruits about to embark, I rashly offered to go with then; my offer was accepted, and I embarked at Leith, with seventeen others, for the Isle of Wight, in July 1806.

The morning was beautiful and refreshing. A fine breeze wafted us from the Roads. The darkness of the preceding night only tended to deepen the gloomy agitation of my mind; but the beauties of the morning scene stole over my soul, and stilled the perturbation of my mind. The violent beat of the pulse at my temples subsided, and I, as it were, awoke from a dream. I turned my eyes, from the beauties of the Forth, to the deck of the vessel on which I stood: I had not yet exchanged words with any of my fellow-recruits; I now inquired of the sergeant, to what regiment I had engaged myself? His answer was, 'To the gallant 71st; you are a noble lad, and shall be an officer.' He ran on in this fulsome cant for some time. I heard him not. Tantallon and the Bass[3] were only a little way from us. We were quickly leaving behind all that was dear to me, and all I ought to regret: the shores of Lothian had vanished; we had passed Dunbar. I was seized with a sudden agitation; a menacing voice seemed to ask, 'What do you here? What is to become of your parents?' The blood forsook my heart; a delirium followed, and I fell on the deck.

I have no recollection of what passed for some days. I was roused out of my lethargy by a bustle over my head. It was the fearful noise of a storm, which had overtaken us in Yarmouth Roads. The looks of despair, and the lamentable cries of the passengers, pierced me. I looked upon myself as the only cause of our present danger, like Jonah, overtaken in my guilty flight. The thought of acknowledging myself the sole cause of the storm more than once crossed my mind. I certainly would have done so, had not the violent rocking of the vessel disqualified me from leaving the bed on which I lay. I was obliged to press my feet against one side, and my shoulder against another, to preserve myself from receiving contusions. Striving to assuage the anguish of my feelings in prayer, I was the only composed person there; all around me were bewailing their fate in tears and lamentations. I had seen nothing of the storm, as the passengers were all kept down below, to prevent their incommoding the seamen. During its continuance, I had made up my mind with regard to my future proceedings. As an atonement for my past misconduct, I resolved to undergo all the dangers and fatigues of a private soldier, for seven years. This limitation of service I was enabled to adopt, by the excellent bill brought into Parliament by the late Mr Windham.[4]

Without further accident, we arrived safe at the Isle of Wight, where I was enlisted, and sworn to serve my king and country faithfully for the space of seven years, for which I received a bounty of eleven guineas.[5] The price thus paid for my liberty was the first money I could ever call my own. Of this sum it required about four pounds to furnish my necessaries, assisted by the sale of my present clothing; of the remainder, I sent five pounds to my parents, with the following letter:

NEWPORT BARRACKS,
Isle of Wight, July 1806.

FATHER, – If a disobedient and undutiful son may still address you by that dear and now much valued name – and my mother! – the blood forsakes my heart, and my hand refuses to move, when I think upon that unhallowed night I left your peaceful roof to follow my foolish and wayward inclinations. O, I have suffered, and must ever suffer, for my guilty conduct. Pardon me! pardon me! I can hardly hope – yet, O, drive me not to despair! – I have doomed myself to seven years' punishment. I made this choice in an hour of shame. I could not appear in Edinburgh after what had happened. Never shall I again do any thing to bring shame upon myself or you. The hope of your pardon and forgiveness alone sustains me. Again I implore pardon on my knees. Would I could lay my head at your feet! then would I not rise till you pronounced my pardon, and raised to your embrace your wretched

THOMAS.

Now I began to drink the cup of bitterness. How different was my situation from what it had been! Forced from bed at five o'clock each morning, to get all things ready for drill; then drilled for three hours with the most unfeeling rigour, and often beat by the sergeant for the faults of others. I, who had never been crossed at home – I, who never knew fatigue, was now fainting under it. This I bore without a murmur, as I had looked to it in my engagement. My greatest sufferings were where I had not expected them.

I could not associate with the common soldiers; their habits made me shudder. I feared an oath – they never spoke without one: I could not drink – they loved liquor: They gamed – I knew nothing of play. Thus was I a solitary individual among hundreds. They lost no opportunity of teasing me; 'Saucy Tom,' or 'The distressed Methodist,' were the names they distinguished me by. I had no way of redress, until an event occurred, that gave me, against my will, an opportunity to prove that my spirit was above insult.[6]

A recruit who had joined at the same time with myself, was particularly active in his endeavours to turn me into ridicule. One evening, I was sitting in a side-window, reading. Of an old newspaper he made a fool's cap, and, unperceived by me, placed it upon my head. Fired at the insult, I started up and knocked him down. – 'Clear the room! a ring, a ring! – the Methodist is going to fight!' was vociferated from all sides. Repenting my haste, yet determined not to affront myself, I stood firm, and determined to do my utmost. My antagonist, stunned by the violence of the blow, and surprised at the spirit I displayed, rose slowly, and stood irresolute. I demanded an apology. He began to bluster and threaten, but I saw at once that he was afraid; and, turning from him, said, in a cool decided manner, 'If you dare again insult me, I will chastise you as you deserve; you are beneath my anger.' I again sat down, and resumed my reading, as if nothing had happened.

From this time I was no longer insulted; and I became much esteemed among my fellow-soldiers, who before despised me. Still, I could not associate with them. Their pleasures were repugnant to my feelings.

There was one of my fellow-soldiers, Donald M'Donald, who seemed to take pleasure in my company. We became attached to each other. He came up in the same smack with myself: He was my bedfellow, and became my firm friend. Often would he get himself into altercations on my account. Donald could read and write: this was the sum of his education. He was innocent, and ignorant of the world; only eighteen years of age, and had never been a night from home, before he left his father's house, more than myself. To be a soldier was the height of his ambition. He had come from near Inverness to Edinburgh, on foot, with no other intention than to enlist in the 71st. His father had been a soldier in it, and was now living at home, after being discharged. Donald called it his regiment, and would not have taken the bounty from any other.[7]

Having thus enlisted and been inducted into the army, as soon as 'Thomas' had undergone a brief period of basic training he and nine of his fellow recruits were embarked as a reinforcement for the 71st Highlanders, who were supposedly serving as part of the British garrison at the Cape of Good Hope.

Ordinarily, without a name, tracing him in official documents might be difficult, but in fact he was something of a rare bird. Because the greater part of the 71st had already been captured at Buenos Aires, the ten men belonging to the 11 August 1806 draft to which Thomas belonged were identified quite separately on the regiment's quarterly rolls for some time afterwards.[8] They were, in alphabetical order:

> William Farquhar
> David Faulds
> Edward Floyd
> William Mackee
> James Moody
> Joseph Mulholland
> Joseph Shuder
> Joseph Sinclair
> David Walker
> Peter Yellet

James Todd, it will be observed, was not one of their number, for he was in fact serving with the regiment's 2nd Battalion at the time; yet one of the ten, clearly, must be the Thomas who fought at Buenos Aires, but which one?

Unbeknown to everyone, however, the regiment was actually on the opposite side of the Atlantic. At this point in time Britain was also at war with Spain and Spain's navy had effectively been destroyed in the epic battle of Trafalgar on 21 October 1805. Traditionally Trafalgar has been seen as a resounding victory against the French which removed the threat of invasion once and for all and established Britain's naval superiority for generations to come.

In this Anglo-centric view the presence of the Spanish fleet was simply an incidental factor which served only to inflate the magnitude of the victory. In reality Spain was the real loser of the battle, for the loss of its fleet left its vast American empire invitingly open to attack, and if Britain lacked the resources to do so immediately there were always the colonists themselves. Encouraging unrest in those colonies, if not outright rebellion, was clearly a desirable object in itself and was all the more desirable in the light of a burgeoning trade between Britain and South America which could only improve if Spain and her punitive customs regime were cut out of the picture. However, what really clinched the matter for those actually involved in planning the whole thing was the perception that the province of De La Plata – present-day Uruguay and northern Argentina – was awash with silver. And so without any official authorisation, in June 1806 Admiral Home Popham persuaded Sir David Baird, the British commander at the Cape, to lend his old 71st Highlanders for an unauthorised filibustering expedition to conquer South America.

Popham, and a Colonel William Beresford,[9] duly seized Buenos Aires in June 1806 and at first everything looked very promising, but rather than confine himself to liberating the citizens the gallant Admiral also chose to liberate over a million dollars in silver, which was promptly forwarded to a grateful Treasury by way of justifying his initiative. A suitably mollified Government promptly responded by dispatching further troops to reinforce his success, but in the meantime the Spaniards and the less than revolutionary colonists launched a counter-attack, retaking the city and capturing most of the 71st Highlanders in the process.

SAILS for South America – Arrival at Madeira – Arrival at the Cape of Good Hope, and Account of Cape Town – Arrival at the River La Plata – Situation of the English Army – Battle of Monte Video – Account of the Inhabitants – Introduced to a Spanish priest.

To increase my grief, I was ordered to embark for the Cape of Good Hope, fifteen days after my arrival in the Isle of Wight[10] and before I had received an answer to my letter to my father. If my mind had been at ease, I would have enjoyed this voyage much. We had very pleasant weather, and were not crowded in our berths. There were six soldiers to a berth, and we were at liberty to be on deck all day, if we chose.

The first land I saw, after leaving the Channel, was Porto Santo. It is very low, yet we could distinguish it plainly while we were thirty miles off. It has the appearance of a collection of small hills ending in peaks. In a short time after, we had a most pleasant sight: the island of Madeira, covered with delightful verdure. The view of it calmed me greatly; and I felt just as I had done, the first time I saw the country, after a long illness in which my life was despaired of. How much was that pleasure increased, when we anchored between the Desertas and the island! The weather was beautiful and clear; we lay at a distance of not more than six or seven miles, at most, from the shore. The island is quite unlike Porto Santo. It seems to be one continued mountain, running from east to west, covered with stately trees and verdure. Every spot looked more luxuriant than another. As it is approached from the east, it has the appearance of a crescent, or new moon; the corners pointed towards you.

While we lay there, we had boats alongside, every day, with oranges, lemons, figs, and many other fruits, which we purchased at a rate that surprised us, considering how dearly we had been accustomed to purchase them in England.

As soon as we cast anchor, the health-boat came alongside, to inquire the state of the crew and passengers. This is always done, before any communication is allowed with the island. We had the pleasure to tell them, that there was not a sick person on board; that we only wanted a supply of water, and were to sail as soon as possible.

Funchal is the largest town on the island. It is situated on the north side of the hill, towards the ocean, covering the hill from the summit to the base. The houses reach to the water's edge, and they all look as if they were newly built, they are so white and clean. Another range of hills is seen rising above the one on which the town is built; these are also covered with houses, vineyards, and plantations of fruit-trees. Nothing could be more charming to our eyes, which had ached so long, in looking over a boundless expanse of sea.

Having completed our supply of water, we set sail for the Cape of Good Hope. As we sailed onwards, I was often surprised at the immense number of fishes of all descriptions that played round our vessel. When the weather was calm, fish of every kind, the dolphin, flying fish, &c. were mixed harmlessly together. The shark was seen playing amongst them, and they not in the least alarmed. Small and large, all seemed collected before us to display the beauties and riches of Divine Providence in the great deep. In a dark night, the sea seemed sparkling with fire.

I inquired the cause of this assemblage of fishes, and their tameness, at an old sailor: He informed me, that the cause was the reflection of the copper on the ship's bottom, and that they were never seen unless the vessel was coppered.

It was early in the morning, when we first beheld the land about the Cape of Good Hope. We soon after could distinguish a hill, called the Sugar Loaf; and next reached a low island, called Robben Island. We anchored in Table Bay, and were disembarked next day.

Cape Town lies in a valley, the sides of which rise gently to the foot of the mountains that encompass it on all sides. Those near the town are of a great height. The houses of the town are all coloured white or yellow. They are mostly built of stone, and appear as if they were not a month old, they are so clean. The streets are paved with flag-stones, which, I am told, are brought from India. They are very agreeable in so hot a climate, being very cool.

I expected to see few people here but Dutch; but I found a collection of all the nations in the world. No doubt, the Dutch are the most numerous; but there are a great many Germans, Swiss, French, British, Irish, &c. all very much assimilated to each other. The Dutch have made the French more grave; the French, the Dutch less sedate. Every class of foreigners seems the better for being thus mixed with others. All are equally industrious; all seem happy and content.

I remained only three weeks at the Cape. I was again embarked in an expedition against South America, under Sir Samuel Auchmuty[11] and Brigadier-General Lumley.[12]

We arrived in the River La Plata, in October 1806, when we were informed that the Spaniards had retaken Buenos Ayres, and that our troops only possessed Maldonado, a small space on the side of the river, about five or six miles farther up than Monte Video. On our disembarkation, we found the remains of the army in the greatest want of every necessary belonging to an army, and quite disheartened. On the land side, they were surrounded by about 400 horsemen, who cut off all their foraging parties, and intercepted all supplies. These horsemen were not regular soldiers, but the inhabitants of the country, who had turned out to defend their homes from the enemy.

Soon after our arrival at Maldonado, the Spaniards advanced out of Monte Video to attack us. They were about 600, and had, besides, a number of great guns with them. They came upon us in two columns, the right consisting of cavalry, the left of infantry, and bore so hard upon our out-picquet of 400 men, that Colonel Brown,[13] who commanded our left, ordered Major Campbell,[14] with three companies of the 40th regiment, to its support. These charged the head of the column: the Spaniards stood firm and fought bravely; numbers fell on both sides; but the gallant 40th drove them back with the point of the bayonet. Sir Samuel Auchmuty ordered the rifle corps, and light battalion, to attack the rear of their column, which was done with the utmost spirit. Three cheers were the signal of our onset. The Spaniards fled; and the right column, seeing the fate of their left, set spurs to their horses, and also fled without having shared in the action. There remained in our possession one general, and a great number of prisoners, besides one of their great guns. They left about 300 dead on the field. We had very few wounded prisoners, and these were taken in the pursuit. I saw them carry their people back to the town as soon as they were hurt. Our loss was much less than theirs.

After this action, we saw no more of our troublesome guests, the horsemen, who used to brave us in our lines, and even wound our people in the camp.

This was the first blood I had ever seen shed in battle; – the first time that cannon had roared in my hearing charged with death. I was not yet seventeen years of age, and had not been six months from home. My limbs bending under me with fatigue, in a sultry climate, the musket and accoutrements that I was forced to carry were insupportably oppressive. Still I bore all with invincible patience. During the action, the thought of death never once crossed my mind. After the firing commenced, a still sensation stole over my whole frame, a firm determined torpor, bordering on insensibility. I heard an old soldier answer, to a youth like myself, who inquired what he should do during the battle, 'Do your duty.'

As the battalion to which I belonged returned from the pursuit, we passed, in our way to the camp, over the field of the dead. It was too much for my feelings. I was obliged to turn aside my head from the horrid sight. The birds of prey seemed to contend with those who were burying the slain, for the possession of the bodies. Horrid sight! Men, who, in the morning, exulting strode forth in strength; whose minds, only fettered by their bodies, seemed to feel restraint, now lay shockingly mangled, and a prey to animals – and I had been an assistant in this work of death! I almost wished I had been a victim.

Until the 2nd of November, my fatigue was great: constructing batteries and other works, we were forced to labour night and day. My hands, when I left home, were white and soft; now they were excoriated and brown, and, where they were unbroken, as hard as horn. Often overpowered by fatigue, sleep has sealed my eyes;- I have awoke groaning with thirst, and the intense heat of my hands. It was then I felt, in all its horror, the folly of my former conduct. Bitter was the sigh that acknowledged my punishment was just.

In the storming of Monte Video I had no share. We remained with the camp to protect the rear. While we lay before the town, the shells of the enemy were falling often near where I stood; one, in particular, seemed as if it would fall at our feet. A young officer ran backwards and forwards, as if he would hide himself; an old soldier said to him, with all the gravity of a Turk, 'You need not hide, Sir; if there is any thing there for you, it will find you out.' The young man looked confused, stood to his duty, and I never saw him appear uneasy again, – so soon was he converted to the warrior's doctrine.

We marched into Monte Video the day after the assault, where I remained seven months. It is a most delightful country, were it not so hot. The evening is the only tolerable time of the day. The sea breeze sets in about eight or nine o'clock in the morning, which mitigates the heat a good deal; yet I suffered much. It was now the middle of December. Summer had commenced with all its sweets, on a scale I had no conception of; neither can I convey any idea of it in words. We had the greatest abundance of every article of food, and, as the summer advanced, the choicest fruit, indeed even more than we could consume, and at length we loathed it.

I had been, along with the other youths, appointed to Sir Samuel Auchmuty's guard, as the least fatiguing duty. I would have been comparatively happy, had I known my parents were well, and had pardoned me: the uncertainty of this, and reflections on my past conduct, kept me in a state of continual gloom.

I was billeted upon a young widow, who did all in her power to make me comfortable, alongst with her aged father. Her husband had been slain in the first attack of our troops upon the place, and she remained inconsolable.

During the seven months I remained in Monte Video, she behaved to me like a mother. To her I was indebted for many comforts. Never shall I forget Maria de Parides: she was of a small figure, yet elegant in her appearance. Like the other women of the country, she was very brown, her eyes sparkling, black as jet, her teeth equal and white. She wore her own hair, when dressed, as is the fashion of the country, in plaits down her back. It was very long, and of a glossy black. Her dress was very plain: a black veil covered her head, and her mantilla was tied in the most graceful manner under her chin. This was the common dress of all the women; the only difference was in the colour of their mantillas and shoes. These they often wore of all colours, and sometimes the veil was white. The men wore the cloak and hat of the Spaniards; but many of them had sandals, and a great many wanted both shoes and stockings. The native women were the most uncomely

I ever beheld. They have broad noses, thick hips, and are of very small stature. Their hair, which is long, black, and hard to the feel, they wear frizzled up in front, in the most hideous manner, while it hangs down their backs below the waist. When they dress, they stick in it feathers and flowers, and walk about in all the pride of ugliness. The men are short of stature, stout made, and have large joints. They are brave, but indolent to excess. I have seen them galloping about on horseback, almost naked, with silver spurs on their bare heels, perhaps an old rug upon their shoulders. They fear not pain. I have seen them with hurts ghastly to look at, yet they never seemed to mind them. As for their idleness, I have seen them lie stretched for a whole day, gazing upon the river, and their wives bring them their victuals; and, if they were not pleased with the quantity, they would beat them furiously. This is the only exertion they ever make, readily venting their fury upon their wives. They prefer flesh to any other food, and they eat it almost raw, and in quantities which a European would think impossible.

I had little opportunity of seeing the better sort of Spanish settlers, as they had all left the place before we took it; and, during the siege, those I had any opportunity of knowing were of the poorer sort, who used to visit Maria de Parides and her father, Don Santanos. They are ignorant in the extreme, and very superstitious. Maria told me, with the utmost concern, that the cause of her husband's death was his being bewitched by an old Indian, to whom he had refused some partridges, as he returned from hunting, a few days before the battle. As I became acquainted with the language, I observed many singular traits of character. When Maria, or old Santanos, yawned, they crossed their mouth with the utmost haste, to prevent the Devil going down their throats. If Santanos sneezed, Maria called, 'Jesus!' his answer was, 'Muchas gracias,' 'Many thanks.' – When they knock at any door, they say, 'Ave Maria purissima;' they open at once, as they think no one with an evil intent will use this holy phrase. When they meet a woman they say, 'A sus pies senora,' or, 'Beso los pies de usted,' 'I lay myself at your feet,' or, 'I kiss your feet.' As they part, he says, 'Me tengo a sus pies de usted,' or, 'Baxo de sus pies,' 'I am at your feet,' or, 'Keep me at your feet;' she replies, 'Beso a usted la mano, Cavellero,' 'I kiss your hand, Sir.' When they leave any one, they say, 'Vaya usted con Dios,' or, 'Con la Virgen,' 'May God, (or, the Holy Virgin,) attend you.' When they are angry, it is a common phrase with them. 'Vaya usted con cien mil Demonios,' 'Begone with a hundred thousand devils.' – Maria was concerned that I should be a heretic, and wished much I would change my religion and become a Catholic, as the only means of my salvation. In vain I said to her, 'Muchos caminos al cielo,' 'Many roads to heaven.' There were few priests in the town, as they had thought it better to move off to Buenos Ayres, with the church-plate, &c. before we took the town, than trust to their prayers and our generosity. Maria, however, got one to convert me, as her own father-confessor had gone with the rest. It was in the afternoon, on my return from guard, I first met him. His appearance made an impression on me, much in his favour; he was tall and graceful, and wore his beard, which was gray and full, giving a venerable cast to his face, and softening the wrinkles that time had made in his forehead. Maria introduced me to him as a young man who was willing to receive instruction, and one she wished much to believe in all the doctrines of the Holy Church, that I might not be lost for ever through my unbelief. He then began to say a great deal about the errors of the Protestants, and their undone state, since they had left the true church. The only answer I made was, 'Muchos caminos al cielo.' He shook his head, and said, all heretics were a stubborn sort of people, but begged me to consider of what he said. I answered, certainly I would and we parted friends. Maria was much disappointed at my not being convinced at once; and her father, Santanos, said he had no doubt that I would yet become a good Catholic, and remain with them. I loved them the more for their disinterested zeal: their only wish was for my welfare.

— ◆ —

ARRIVAL of General Whitelock with reinforcements – Departure for Buenos Ayres – Attack of the Town – Unfortunate result – Anecdote of a Sergeant – Generous behaviour of the Spanish priest.

Thus had I passed my time, until the arrival of General Whitelock,[15] with reinforcements, in the beginning of June 1807. It was the middle of winter at Monte Video; the nights were frosty, with now and then a little snow, and great showers of hail as large as beans. In the day, dreadful rains deluged all around. We had sometimes thunder and lightning. One night in particular, the whole earth seemed one continued blaze; the mountain, on the side of which the town is built, re-echoed the thunder, as if it would rend in pieces. The whole inhabitants flocked to the churches, or kneeled in the streets.

On the arrival of the reinforcements, we were formed into a brigade, along with the light companies of the 36th, 38th, 40th, 87th, and four companies of the 95th regiments. On the 28th June, we assembled near Ensenada de Barragon, with the whole army, and commenced our march towards Buenos Ayres.

The country is almost all level, and covered with long clover that reached to our waists, and large herds of bullocks and horses, which seemed to run wild. The weather was very wet. For days I had not a dry article on my body. We crossed many morasses in our march, in one of which I lost my shoes, and was under the necessity of marching the rest of the way barefooted. We passed the river at a ford called Passorico, under the command of Major-General Gower.[16] Here we drove back a body of the enemy. We were next day joined by General Whitelock, and the remainder of the army. Upon his joining us, the line was formed by Sir Samuel Auchmuty on the left, stretching towards a convent called the Recoletta, distant from the left about two miles. Two regiments were stationed on the right. Brigadier-General Crawford's brigade[17] occupied the centre, and possessed the principal avenues to the town, which was distant from the great square and fort three miles. Three regiments extended towards the Residenta, on the right. The town and suburbs are built in squares of about 140 yards on each side; and all the houses are flat on the top for the use of the inhabitants, who go upon them to enjoy the cool of the evening. These, we were told, they meant to occupy with their slaves, and fire down upon us as we charged through the streets. From the disposition of our army, the town was nearly surrounded. We remained under arms on the morning of the 5th of July, waiting the order to advance. Judge our astonishment when the word was given to march without ammunition, with fixed bayonets only. 'We are betrayed,' was whispered through the ranks. 'Mind your duty, my lads onwards, onwards, Britain for ever!' were the last words I heard our noble Captain Brookman utter. He fell as we entered the town. Onwards we rushed, carrying every thing before us, scrambling over ditches, and other impediments which the inhabitants had placed in our way. At the corner of every street, and flanking all the ditches, they had placed cannon that thinned our ranks every step we took. Still onwards we drove, up one street, down another, until we came to the church of St Domingo, where the colours of the 71st regiment had been placed, as a trophy, over the shrine of the Virgin Mary. We made a sally into it, and took them from that disgraceful resting place, where they had remained ever since the surrender of General Beresford to General Liniers. Now we were going to sally out in triumph. The Spaniards had not been idle. The entrances of the church were barricaded, and cannon placed at each entrance. We were forced to surrender, and were marched to prison.

It was there I first learned the complete failure of our enterprise. During the time we were charging through the streets, many of our men made sallies into the houses in search of plunder; and many were encumbered with it at the time of our surrender. One sergeant of the 38th had made a longish hole in his wooden canteen, like that over the money-drawer in the counter of a retail shop; into it he slipped all the money he could lay his hands upon. As he came out of a house he had been ransacking, he was shot through the head. In his fall the canteen burst, and a great many doubloons ran in all directions on the street. Then commenced a scramble for the money, and about eighteen men were shot, grasping at the gold they were never to enjoy. They even snatched it from their dying companions, although they themselves were to be in the same situation the next moment.

We were all searched, and every article that was Spanish taken from us; but we were allowed to keep the rest. During the search, one soldier, who had a good many doubloons, put them into his Camp-kettle, with flesh and water above them; placed all upon a fire, and kept them safe. There were about one hundred of us, who had been taken in the church, marched out of prison to be shot, unless we produced a gold crucifix of great value, that was amissing. We stood in a large circle of Spaniards and Indians. Their levelled pieces and savage looks gave us little to hope, unless the crucifix was produced. It was found on the ground on the spot where we stood; but it was not known who had taken it. The troops retired and we were allowed to go back to prison without further molestation.

Four days after we were made prisoners, the good priest I had conversed with in the house of Maria de Parides, came to me in prison, and offered to obtain my release, if I would only say that I would, at any future time, embrace the Catholic faith. He held out many inducements.

34

I thanked him kindly for his offer, but told him it was impossible I ever could. He said, 'I have done my duty as a servant of God; now I will do it as a man.' He never again spoke to me of changing my religion; yet he visited me every day with some comfort or another.

Donald M'Donald was quite at home all the time we had been in South America. He was a good Catholic, and much caressed by the Spaniards. He attended mass regularly, bowed to all processions, and was in their eyes every thing a good Catholic ought to be. He often thought of remaining at Buenos Ayres, under the protection of the worthy priest; he had actually agreed to do so, when the order for our release arrived. We were to join General Whitelock on the next day, after fourteen days' confinement. Donald was still wavering, yet most inclined to stay. I sung to him, 'Lochaber no more!' the tears started into his eyes – he dashed them off – 'Na, na! I canna stay, I'd maybe return to Lochaber nae mair.' The good priest was hurt at his retracting his promise, yet was not offended. He said, 'It is natural. I once loved Spain above all the other parts of the world; but – ' here he checked himself, gave us his blessing, and ten doubloons a piece, and left us. We immediately, upon our release, set out on our return to Britain, and had an agreeable and quick passage, in which nothing particular occurred.

2

Safely returned from South America Thomas was now about to embark upon the next stage of his adventures, for there had been a dramatic reversal of alliances. Portugal, a long-standing ally of Britain had been invaded by the French in November and December of 1807 with the active assistance of Spain. The takeover of the country was quickly accomplished and its royal family fled almost at the very outset to take up a rather agreeable exile in Brazil. However, in the following March, French troops supposedly en route for Portugal suddenly seized the Spanish fortresses they were passing through and Napoleon's brother Joseph was elevated to the throne. Viewed rationally, exchanging a Bourbon for a Bonaparte was a decidedly progressive move, but instead the Spaniards failed to be suitably grateful and in May rose up in revolt, precipitating a war of independence which would rage for the next seven years. As the enemy of France, Britain thus became the ally of Spain and on 1 August 1808 a British expeditionary force led by Sir Arthur Wellesley landed in Portugal.

*ARRIVAL at Cork – Correspondence with his brother –
Sails for Portugal, with an expedition under Sir Arthur
Wellesley – Battle of Roleia – Description of Vimeira –
Battle of Vimeira – Behaviour of the peasants after the
battle.*

It was on the 25th December 1807, after an absence of
seventeen months from Britain, that I landed at the Cove
of Cork in Ireland. A thrill of joy ran through my whole
body, and prompted a fervid inward ejaculation to God,
who had sustained me through so many dangers, and
brought me to a place where I might hear if my parents
had pardoned me, or if my misconduct had shortened the
period of their lives. The uncertainty of this embittered
all my thoughts, and gave additional weight to all my
fatigues. How differently did the joy of our return act
upon my fellow-soldiers! – to them it was a night of
riot and dissipation. Immediately on our arrival, our
regiment was marched to Middleton Barracks, where we
remained one month; during which time I wrote to my
father, and sent him the amount of the ten doubloons I
had received from the good priest. In the course of post
I received the following letter, enclosed in one from my
brother. It had been returned to them by the post-office
at the Isle of Wight.

Edinburgh, 5th August, 1806.

DEAR THOMAS,
We received your letter from the Isle of Wight, which gave
us much pleasure. I do not mean to add to your sorrows by
any reflection upon what is past, as you are now sensible

of your former faults, and the cruelty of your desertion. Let it be a lesson to you in future. It had nearly been our deaths. Your mother, brothers, and myself, searched in every quarter that night you left us; but it pleased God we should not find you. Had we only known you were alive, we would have been happy. We praise God you are safe, and send you our forgiveness and blessings. The money you have sent, we mean to assist to purchase your discharge, if you will leave the army and come to us again. You say you have made a vow to remain seven years. It was rash to do so, if you have vowed solemnly. Write us on receipt of this, that I may know what course to pursue.

YOUR LOVING PARENT.

Edinburgh, 5th January 1808.

DEAR BROTHER,

We received your letter with joy. It has relieved our minds from much uneasiness; but, alas! he who would have rejoiced most, is no more. My heart bleeds for you, on receipt of this; but, on no account, I beseech you, think your going away caused his death. You know he had been long badly, before you left us; and it pleased God to take him to his reward, shortly after your departure. He received your letter two days before his death. He was, at the time, propped up in bed. It was a beautiful forenoon. William and myself were at his bedside; Jean and our dear mother each held a hand. Our father said in his usual manner, 'My dear children, I feel the time at hand, in which I am to bid adieu to this scene of troubles. I would go to my final abode content and happy, would it please God to let me hear of Thomas; if dead, that our ashes might mingle together; if alive, to convey to him my pardon and blessings; for ere now, I feel conscious he mourns for his faults.' As he spoke, your letter arrived. He opened it himself; and, as he read, his face beamed with joy, and the tears ran down his cheeks. 'Gallant, unfortunate boy, may God bless and forgive you, as I do.' He gave me the letter to read to my mother, aloud. While I read it, he seemed to pray fervently. He then desired me to write to you, as he would dictate. This letter was returned to us again. I now send it to you under cover of this. Your mother is well, and sends you her blessings; but wishes you to leave the army, and come home. The money you sent just now, and the five pounds before, will purchase your discharge. Send us the happy intelligence you will do so. I remain,

YOUR LOVING BROTHER.

On receipt of this letter, I became unfit to do or think on any thing but the fatal effects of my folly. I fell into a lowness of spirits, that continued with me until my arrival in Spain; when the fatigue and hardship I was forced to undergo, roused me from my lethargy.

I was now more determined to remain with the army, to punish myself, than ever. This I wrote to my brother, and desired him to make my mother as comfortable as possible with the money I had sent.

We remained only one month in Middleton barracks, when we were again marched to Cork barracks, where I remained until the 27th June 1808, when I was embarked with, the troops on an expedition under Sir Arthur Wellesley, consisting of nine regiments of infantry. We remained at anchor until the 12th July, when we set sail for the coast of Portugal, where we arrived on the 29th July, at Mondego Bay.

We began to disembark on the 1st of August. The weather was so rough and stormy, that we were not all landed until the 5th. On our leaving the ships, each man got four pound of biscuit, and four pound of salt beef cooked on board. We marched, for twelve miles, up to the knees in sand, which caused us to suffer much from thirst; for the marching made it rise and cover us. We lost four men of our regiment, who died of thirst. We buried them where they fell. At night we came to our camp ground, in a wood, where we found plenty of water, to us more acceptable than any thing besides on earth. We here built large huts, and remained four days. We again commenced our march alongst the coast, towards Lisbon. In our advance, we found all the villages deserted, except by the old and destitute, who cared not what became of them.

On the 13th, there was a small skirmish between the French and our cavalry, after which the French retired. On the 14th, we reached a village called Alcobaco, which the French had left the night before. Here were a great many wine stores, that had been broken open by the French. In a large wine cask, we found a French soldier, drowned, with all his accoutrements.

On the morning of the 17th, we were under arms an hour before day. Half an hour after sunrise, we observed the enemy in a wood. We received orders to retreat. Having fallen back about two miles, we struck to the right, in order to come upon their flank, whilst the 9th, 29th, and 5th battalion of the 60th, attacked them in front.[1] They had a very strong position on a hill. The 29th advanced up the hill, not perceiving an ambush of the enemy, which they had placed on each side of the road. As soon as the 29th was right between them, they gave a volley, which killed or wounded every man in the grenadier company, except seven.[2] Unmindful of their loss, they drove on, and carried the intrenchments. The engagement lasted until about four o'clock, when the enemy gave way. We continued the pursuit, till darkness put a stop to it. The 71st had only one man killed and one wounded. We were manoeuvring all day, to turn their flank; so that our fatigue was excessive, though our loss was but small. This was the battle of Roleia, a small town at the entrance of a hilly part of the country.

We marched the whole of the 18th and 19th without meeting any resistance. On the 19th, we encamped at the village of Vimeira, and took up a position alongst a range of mountains.

On the 20th, we marched out of our position to cover the disembarkation of four regiments, under General Anstruther.[3] We saw a few French cavalry, who kept manoeuvring, but did not offer to attack us.

On the 21st, we were all under arms an hour before day-break. After remaining some time we were dismissed, with orders to parade again at 10 o'clock, to attend divine service for this was a Sabbath morning. How unlike the Sabbaths I was wont to enjoy! Had it not been for the situation in which I had placed myself, I could have enjoyed it much.

Vimeira is situated in a lovely valley, through which the small river Maceira winds, adding beauty to one of the sweetest scenes, surrounded on all sides by mountains and the sea, from which the village is distant about three miles. There is a deep ravine that parts the heights, over which the Lourinha road passes. We were posted on these mountains, and had a complete view of the valley below. I here, for a time, indulged in one of the most pleasing reveries I had enjoyed since I left home. I was seated upon the side of a mountain, admiring the beauties beneath. I thought of home: Arthur's Seat, and the level between it and the sea, all stole over my imagination. I became lost in contemplation, and was happy for a time.

Soon my day-dream broke, and vanished from my sight. The bustle around was great. There was no trace of a day of rest. Many were washing their linen in the river, others cleaning their firelocks; every man was engaged in some employment. In the midst of our preparation for divine service, the French columns began to make their appearance on the opposite hills. 'To arms, to arms!' was beat, at half-past eight o'clock. Every thing was packed up as soon as possible, and left on the camp ground.

We marched out two miles, to meet the enemy, formed line, and lay under cover of a hill, for about an hour, until they came to us. We gave them one volley, and three cheers – three distinct cheers. Then all was as still as death. They came upon us, crying and shouting, to the very point of our bayonets. Our awful silence and determined advance they could not stand. They put about, and fled without much resistance. At this charge we took thirteen guns, and one General.[4]

We advanced into a hollow, and formed again: then returned in file, from the right in companies, to the rear. The French came down upon us again. We gave them another specimen of a charge, as effectual as our first, and pursued them three miles.

In our first charge, I felt my mind waver; a breathless sensation came over me. The silence was appalling. I looked alongst the line: It was enough to assure me. The steady determined scowl of my companions assured my heart, and gave me determination. How unlike the noisy advance of the French! It was in this second charge, our piper, George Clark, was wounded in the groin.[5] We remained at our advance, until sunset; then retired to our camp ground. The ground was so unequal, that I saw little of this battle, which forced the French to evacuate Portugal.

On my return from the pursuit at Monte Video, the birds of prey were devouring the slain. Here I beheld a sight, for the first time, even more horrible; the peasantry prowling about, more ferocious than the beasts and birds of prey, finishing the work of death, and carrying away whatever they thought worthy of their grasp. Avarice and revenge were the causes of these horrors. No fallen Frenchman, that showed the least signs of life, was spared. They even seemed pleased with mangling the bodies. When light failed them, they kindled a great fire, and remained around it all night, shouting like as many savages. My sickened fancy felt the same as if it were witnessing a feast of cannibals.

Next morning we perceived a column of the enemy upon the sand-hills. We were all in arms to receive them, but it turned out to be a flag of truce. We returned to our old camp ground, where we remained three days, during the time the terms of a capitulation were arranging. We then got orders to march to Lisbon. On our arrival there, the French flag was flying on all the batteries and forts. We were encamped outside of the town; and marched in our guards, next day, to take possession, and relieve all the French guards. At the same time the French flag was hauled down, and we hoisted, in its stead, the Portuguese standard.[6]

We remained in camp until the day the French were to embark. We were then marched in, to protect them from the inhabitants but, notwithstanding all we could do, it was not in our power to hinder some of their sick from being murdered. The Portuguese were so much enraged at our interference in behalf of the French, that it was unsafe for two or three soldiers to be seen alone. The French had given the Portuguese much cause to hate them; and the latter are not a people who can quickly forgive an injury, or let slip any means of revenge, however base.

— ♦ —

MARCHED to Escurial – Retreat to Salamanca – Disappointment of our soldiers at not being allowed to attack the enemy.

On the 27th October we quitted Lisbon, and marched to Abrantes, where we remained fourteen days. Then we marched to Camponia, and remained there for an order to enter Spain.[7]

The first place we arrived at in Spain was Badajos where we were very kindly treated by the inhabitants and Spanish soldiers. We remained there about a fortnight, when the division commanded by General Sir John Hope,[8] to which I belonged, received orders to march towards Madrid. We halted at Escurial, about seven leagues from Madrid, and remained there five days; but were at length forced to retreat to Salamamca.

Two days before our arrival at Salamanca, we were forced to form ourselves into a square, to repel the attacks of the enemy; and in that position we remained all night. It was one of the severest nights of cold I ever endured in my life. At that time we wore long hair, formed into a club at the back of our heads. Mine was frozen to the ground in the morning; and, when I attempted to rise, my limbs refused to support me for some time. I felt the most excruciating pains over all my body, before the blood began to circulate.

We marched forty-seven miles this day, before encamping, and about nine miles to a town next morning, where the inhabitants were very kind to us. They brought out, into the market-place, large tub-fuls of accadent, (a liquor much used in Spain), that we might take our pleasure of it; and every thing they had that we stood in need of. This day we were under the necessity of burying six guns, on account of the horses failing, being quite worn down by fatigue. The head-quarters of the army were at Salamanca. Our division was quartered three leagues from it, at Alva de Tormes.

On the 14th of December we advanced to a place called Torro. The roads were bad; the weather very severe; all around was covered with snow. Our fatigue was dreadful, and our sufferings almost more than we could endure.

On the 24th of December our head-quarters were at Sahagun. Every heart beat with joy. We were all under arms, and formed to attack the enemy. Every mouth breathed hope: 'We will beat them to pieces, and have our ease, and enjoy ourselves,' said my comrades. I even preferred any short struggle however severe, to the dreadful way of life we were, at this time, pursuing. With heavy hearts we received orders to retire to our quarters: 'And won't we be allowed to fight? sure we'd beat them,' said an Irish lad near me; 'by Saint Patrick, we beat them so easy, the General means to march us to death, and fight them after!'

Next morning we fell back upon Majorga, on the road to Benevente.

— ◆ —

COMMENCEMENT of the retreat to Corunna – Indignant feelings of the soldiers – Duke of Ossuna's Palace at Benevente much destroyed – Skirmish at Benevente – Arrival at Astorga, and account of the situation of General Romana's army.

On the 25th, Christmas day, we commenced our route for the sea-coast, melancholy and dejected, sinking under extreme cold and fatigue, as if the very elements had conspired against us: then commenced the first day of our retreat.

On the 26th, it rained the whole day, without intermission. The soil here is of a deep rich loam, and the roads were knee-deep with clay. To form a regular march was impossible, yet we kept in regiments; but our sufferings were so great, that many of our troops lost all their natural activity and spirits, and became savage in their dispositions. The idea of running away from an enemy we had beat with so much ease at Vimeira, without even firing a shot, was too galling to their feelings. Each spoke to his fellow, even in common conversation, with bitterness; rage flashing from their eyes, on the most trifling occasions of disagreement.

The poor Spaniards had little to expect from such men as these, who blamed them for their inactivity. Every one found at home was looked upon as a traitor to his country. 'The British are here to fight for the liberty of Spain, and why is not every Spaniard under arms and fighting? The cause is not ours; and are we to be the only sufferers?' Such was the common language of the soldiers; and from these feelings pillage and outrage naturally arose. The conduct of the men, in this respect, called forth, on the 27th, a severe reprimand from the Commander-in-Chief.

We halted at Benevente for one night. Just as the last division of our army entered into the town, the drums beat to arms. Every man was on the alert, and at his post, in an instant. The cavalry poured out at the gates to meet the enemy; but the French did not like the manner and spirit that appeared amongst us. They retired from the heights, and we endeavoured to pass the night in the best manner in our power.

28th, the Spaniards now gave us no assistance, save what was enforced. The Duke of Ossuna has here a castle surpassing any thing I had ever seen. It was such, on our arrival, as I have read the description of in books of fairy tales. I blush for our men; I would blame them too; alas! how can I, when I think upon their dreadful situation, fatigued and wet, shivering, perishing with cold? – no fuel to be got, not even straw to lie upon. Can men in such a situation admire the beauties of art? Alas! only so far as they relieve his cruel and destroying wants. Every thing that would burn was converted into fuel, and even the fires were placed against the walls, that they might last longer and burn better. Many of our men slept all night wrapt in rich tapestry, which had been torn down to make bed-clothes.

Scarce was our rear-guard within the town, ere the alarm was sounded. We rushed to our posts, pushing the inhabitants out of our way. Women and children crowded the streets, wringing their hands, and calling upon their saints for protection. The opposite plain was covered with fugitives. The French, as usual, liked not the spirit with which we formed, and the ardour with which our cavalry issued from the gates. They were content to look upon us from the neighbouring heights. The bridges were ordered to be destroyed, which was done before day. That over the Esla had been destroyed to little purpose, as a ford was found only 300 yards farther down the river. The picquets hastened thither, and were skirmishing with four squadrons of the Imperial Guards, who had already formed on the bank. The 10th Hussars were sent for. On their arrival, General Stewart, with them and the picquets, charged and drove the Imperial Guard into the river. They crossed in the utmost confusion, but formed on the opposite bank. Some pieces of artillery that had been placed at the bridge soon dispersed them. General Lefebvre, commander of the Imperial Guards, and seventy prisoners, were the fruits of this action. We were told by the Spaniards, that Buonaparte saw this affair from the heights.

On the 30th, we reached Astorga, which we were led to believe was to be our resting-place, and the end of our fatigues. Here we found the army of General Romana. I can convey no description of it in words. It had more the appearance of a large body of peasants, driven from their homes, famished, and in want of every thing, than a regular army. Sickness was making dreadful havoc amongst them. It was whispered we were to make a stand here. This was what we all wished, though none believed. We had been told so at Benevente; but our movements had not the smallest appearance of a retreat, in which we were to face about and make a stand; they were more like a shameful flight.

— ♦ —

SUFFERINGS of the army between Astorga and Villa Franca — Cruelty of the French — March from Villa Franca to Castro — March to Lugo — Bravery of the stragglers — Affecting occurrence — Skirmishes at Lugo — Relaxed state of discipline, and its consequences.

From Astorga to Villa Franca de Bierzo, is about sixty miles. From Salamanca to Astorga may be called the first and easiest part of this tragedy, in which we endured many privations and much fatigue; from Astorga to Villa Franca, the second, and by far the more severe part. Here we suffered misery without a glimpse of comfort. At Astorga there were a great many pairs of shoes destroyed. Though a fourth of the army were in want of them, and I amongst the rest, yet they were consumed alongst with the other stores in the magazines.

The first sixteen miles the road lay wholly up the mountain, to the summit of Foncebadon; and the country was open. At this time it was a barren waste of snow. At the top of the mountain is a pass, which is one of the strongest, they say, in Europe. It is about eight or nine miles long. All the way through this pass the silence was only interrupted by the groans of the men, who, unable to proceed farther, laid themselves down in despair to perish in the snow; or where the report of a pistol told the death of a horse, which had fallen down, unable to proceed. I felt an unusual listlessness steal over me. Many times have I said, 'These men who have resigned themselves to their fate, are happier than I. What have I to struggle for? Welcome death! happy deliverer!' These thoughts passed in my mind involuntarily. Often have I been awakened out of this state of torpor by my constant friend, Donald, when falling out of the line of march to lie down in despair. The rain poured in torrents; the melted snow was half knee-deep in many places, and stained by the blood that flowed from our wounded and bruised feet. To add to our misery, we were forced, by turns, to drag the baggage. This was more than human nature could sustain. Many waggons were abandoned, and much ammunition destroyed. Our arrival at Villa Franca closed the second act of our tragedy.

From Villa Franca we set out on the 2nd January 1809. What a New-year's day had we passed! Drenched with rain, famished with cold and hunger, ignorant when our misery was to cease. This was the most dreadful period of my life. How differently did we pass our hogmanay, from the manner our friends were passing theirs, at home? Not a voice said, 'I wish you a happy new year;' each seemed to look upon his neighbour as an abridgment to his own comforts. His looks seemed to say, 'One or other of the articles you wear would be of great use to me; your shoes are better than those I possess: if you were dead, they would be mine!'

Before we set out there were more magazines destroyed. Great numbers would not leave the town, but concealed themselves in the wine cellars, which they had broken open, and were left there; others, after we were gone, followed us. Many came up to the army dreadfully cut and wounded by the French cavalry, who rode through the long lines of these lame, defenceless wretches, slashing among them as a school-boy does among thistles. Some of them, faint and bleeding, were forced to pass along the line as a warning to others. Cruel warning! Could the urgency of the occasion justify it? There was something in the appearance of these poor, emaciated, lacerated wretches, that sickened me to look upon. Many around me said, 'Our commanders are worse than the French: will they not even let us die in peace, if they cannot help us?' Surely this was one way to brutalize the men, and render them familiar to scenes of cruelty.

Dreadful as our former march had been, it was from Villa Franca that the march of death may be said to have begun. On, the day after we left that place, we were attacked by the French, but drove them back, and renewed our forlorn march.

From Villa Franca to Castro, is one continued toil up Monte del Cebiero. It was one of the sweetest scenes I ever beheld, could our eyes have enjoyed any thing that did not minister to our wants. There was nothing to sustain our famished bodies, or shelter them from the rain or snow. We were either drenched with rain or crackling with ice. Fuel we could find none. The sick and wounded that we had been still enabled to drag with us in the wagons, were now left to perish in the snow. The road was one line of bloody foot-marks, from the sore feet of the men; and, on its sides, lay the dead and the dying. Human nature could do no more. – Donald M'Donald, the hardy Highlander, began to fail. He, as well as myself, had long been barefooted and lame; he that had encouraged me to proceed, now himself lay down to die. For two days he had been almost blind, and unable, from a severe cold, to hold up his head. We sat down together; not a word escaped our lips. We looked around – then at each other, and closed our eyes. – We felt there was no hope. – We would have given in charge a farewell to our friends; but who was to carry it? There were, not far from us, here and there, above thirty in the same situation with ourselves. There was nothing but groans, mingled with execrations, to be heard, between the pauses of the wind. – I attempted to pray, and recommend myself to God; but my mind was so confused I could not arrange my ideas. I almost think I was deranged. We had not sat half an hour; sleep was stealing upon me, when I perceived a bustle around me. It was an advanced party of the French. Unconscious of the action I started upon my feet, levelled my musket, which I had still retained, fired, and formed with the other stragglers. The French faced about and left us. There were more of them than of us. The action, and the approach of danger, in a shape which we had it in our power to repel, roused out dormant feelings, and we joined at Castro.

From Castro to Lugo is about forty-eight miles, where we were promised two days rest. Why should I continue longer this melancholy narrative? Donald fell out again from sickness, and I from lameness and fatigue. When the French arrived, we formed with the others as before, and they fell back. I heard them, more than once, say, as they turned from the points of our bayonets, that they would rather face a hundred fresh Germans, than ten dying English, – so great was the alarm we caused in them. How mortifying to think, at these moments, that we were suffering all our misery, flying from an enemy who dared not fight us, and fled from us, poor wretches as we were! How unaccountable was our situation! None could be more galling to out feelings. While we ran, they pursued: the moment we faced about, they halted. If we advanced, they retired. Never had we fought but with success; never were we attacked but we forced them to retire. 'Let us all unite, whether our officers will or not, and annihilate these French cowards, and show our country it is not our fault that we run thus; let us secure our country from disgrace, and take a sweet revenge.' This was the language of the more spirited men, and in it the others joined, from a hope of relieving their miseries.

With feelings such as these, with a gradual increase of sufferings, we struggled onwards. Towards the close of this journey my mind became unfit for any minute observation. I only marked what I myself was forced to encounter. How I was sustained I am unable to conceive. My life was misery. Hunger, cold, and fatigue, had deprived death of all its horrors. My present sufferings I felt; what death was, I could only guess. 'I will endure every thing, in hope of living to smooth the closing years of my mother's life, and atone for my unkindness. Merciful God! support me.' These ejaculations were always the close of my melancholy musing; after which I felt a new invigoration, though, many times, my reflections were broken short by scenes of horror that came in my way. One, in particular, I found, after I came home, had been much talked of.

After we had gained the summit of Monte del Castro, and were descending, I was roused by a crowd of soldiers. My curiosity prompted me to go to it; I knew it must be no common occurrence that could attract their sympathy. Judge of the feelings which I want words to express. In the centre lay a woman, young and lovely, though cold in death, and a child, apparently about six or seven months old, attempting to draw support from the breast of its dead mother. Tears filled every eye, but no one had the power to aid. While we stood around, gazing on the interesting object, then on each other, none offered to speak, each heart was so full. At length one of General Moore's staff-officers came up, and desired the infant to be given to him. He rolled it in his cloak, amidst the blessings of every spectator. Never shall I efface the benevolence of his look from my heart, when he said, 'Unfortunate infant, you will be my future care.'

From the few remaining wagons we had been able to bring with us, women and children, who had hitherto sustained without perishing all our aggravated sufferings, were, every now and then, laid out upon the snow, frozen to death. An old tattered blanket, or some other piece of garment, was all the burial that was given them. The solders who perished lay uncovered until the next fall of snow, or heavy drift, concealed their bodies.

Amidst scenes like these, we arrived at Lugo. Here we were to have obtained two days' rest; but fate was not yet weary of enjoying our miseries. On our arrival I tried all in my power to find a place for Donald. The best I could find was a bake-house. He lay down in one of the baking-troughs; I put a sack over him. In two minutes the steam began to rise out of the trough in a continued cloud; he fell asleep, and I went in search of some refreshment. I was not half an hour away, when I returned with a little bread; he was still asleep, and as dry as a bone: I was wet as mire. I felt inclined more than once to wake him; I did not, but lay down on a sack, and fell asleep. I awoke before him, quite dry. There were three or four more, lying down on the floor beside me, asleep. My haversack had been rifled while I slept, and my little store of bread was gone. It was vain to complain; I had no resource. Cautiously, I examined those around me asleep, but found nothing. Again I sallied forth; and, to my great joy, I saw a soldier lying unable to rise, he was so drunk. His haversack seemed pretty full: I went to him, and found in it a large piece of beef, and some bread. I scrupled not to appropriate them to myself. I hastened back to Donald, and we had a good meal together. I felt stronger, and Donald was in better spirits.

The bridges between Villa Franca and Lugo had been imperfectly destroyed. The French made their appearance on the 5th of January, and took up a position opposite to our rear guard; a small valley only dividing them from it. This night we remained standing in the fields until day broke; our arms piled. The sky was one continued expanse of stars; not a cloud to be seen, and the frost was most intense. Words fail me to express what we suffered from the most dreadful cold. We alternately went to the calm side of each other, to be sheltered from the Wind. In this manner, when day at length broke upon us, we had retrograded over two fields from the spot where we had piled our arms. Many had lain down, through the night, overcome by sleep, from which the last trumpet only will awaken them.

On the 6th, the enemy attacked our out-posts but were received by our fatigued and famished soldiers with as much bravery as if they had passed the night in comfortable barracks. They repulsed the French in every assault. The sound of the battle roused our drooping hearts – 'Revenge or death!' said my comrades, a savage joy glistening in their eyes. But the day closed without any attack farther on either side.

On the 7th they came upon us again, and were more quickly repulsed than on the day before. From the first moment of the attack, and as long as the French were before us, discipline was restored, and the officers were as punctually obeyed as if we had been on parade at home. We felt not our sufferings; so anxious were we to end them by a victory, which we were certain of obtaining. But Soult seemed to know our spirits better than our own commanders; and, after these two last samples, kept a respectful distance. We stood to our arms until the evening, the enemy in front, amidst snow, rain, and storms. Fires were then lighted, and we commenced our retreat after dark.

Before our reserve left Lugo, general orders were issued, warning and exhorting us to keep order, and to march together; but, alas! how could men observe order amidst such sufferings! or men, whose feet were naked and sore, keep up with men who, being more fortunate, had better shoes and stronger constitutions? The officers, in many points, suffered as much as the men. I have seen officers of the guards, and others, worth thousands, with pieces of old blankets wrapt round their feet and legs; the men pointing, at them, with a malicious satisfaction, saying, 'There goes three thousand a-year;' or, 'There goes the prodigal son on his return to his father, cured of his wanderings.' Even in the midst of all our sorrows, there was a bitterness of spirit, a savageness of wit, that made a jest of its own miseries.

The great fault of our soldiers, at this time. was an inordinate desire for spirits of any kind. They sacrificed their life and safety for drink, in many ways; for they lay down intoxicated upon the snow, and slept the sleep of death; or staggering behind, were overtaken and cut down by the merciless French soldiers: the most favourable event was to be taken prisoners. So great was their propensity to drown their misery in liquor, that we were often exposed to cold and rain for a whole night, in order that we might be kept from the wine-stores of a neighbouring town.

Why should I detain the reader longer on our march? – every day of which was like the day that was past, save in our inability to contend with our hardships.

CHAPTER 2

—◆—

ARRIVAL at Corunna – Destruction of our horses on the beach – Battle of Corunna – Noble conduct of the Spaniards – Arrival in England, and kindness of the people – Sails with the expedition to Walcheren – Description of the bombardment of Flushing - Sally under Colonel Pack into one of the enemy's batteries – Takes the fever, and is sent back to England – Melancholy Discovery at the hospital.

We arrived at Corunna on the 11th January 1809. How shall I describe my sensations at the first sight of the ocean! I felt all my former despondency drop from my mind. My galled feet trod lighter on the icy road. Every face near me seemed to brighten up. Britain and the Sea are two words which cannot be disunited. The sea and home appeared one and the same. We were not cast down at there being no transports or ships of war there. They had been ordered to Vigo, but they were hourly expected.

On the 13th, the French made their appearance on the opposite side of the river Mero. They took up a position near a village called Perillo, on the left bank, and occupied the houses along the river. We could perceive their numbers hourly increasing.

On the 14th, they commenced a cannonade on our position; but our artillery soon forced them to withdraw their guns, and fall back. On this day, our friends, the tars, made their appearance; and all was bustle, preparing for embarkation. The whole artillery was embarked, save seven six-pounders and one howitzer, which were placed in line, and four Spanish guns, which were kept as a reserve. Our position was such, that we could not use many guns. The sick and dismounted cavalry were sent on board with all expedition. I supported my friend Donald, who was now very weak, and almost blind.

On my return to the camp, I witnessed a most moving scene. The beach was covered with dead horses, and resounded with the reports of the pistols that were carrying this havoc amongst them. The animals, as if warned by the dead bodies of their fellows, appeared frantic, neighed and screamed in the most frightful manner. Many broke loose, and galloped along the beach, with their manes erect, and their mouths wide open.

Our preparations continued until the 16th, when every thing was completed, and we were to begin our embarkation at four o'clock. About mid-day we were all under arms, when intelligence arrived that the French were advancing. We soon perceived them pouring down upon our right wing; our advanced picquets had commenced firing. The right had a bad position; yet, if we lost it, our ruin was inevitable. Lord William Bentinck's brigade, composed of the 4th, 42nd, and 50th, had the honour of sustaining it, against every effort of the French, although the latter had every advantage in numbers and artillery. They commenced a heavy fire, from eleven great guns placed in a most favourable manner on the hill. Two strong columns advanced, on the right wing; the one along the road, the other skirting its edges: a third advanced, on the centre; a fourth approached slowly, on the left; while a fifth remained half way down the hill, in the same direction, to take advantage of the first favourable moment. It was at this time that Sir David Baird[9] had his arm shattered.

The space between the two lines was much intercepted by stone walls and hedges. It was perceived by Sir John Moore, as the two lines closed, that the French extended a considerable way beyond the right flank of the British; and a strong body of them were seen advancing up the valley, to turn it. One half of the fourth was ordered to fall back, and form an obtuse angle with the other half. This was done as correctly as could be wished, and a severe flanking fire commenced upon the advancing French. The 50th, after climbing over an enclosure, got right in front of the French, charged, and drove them out of the village of Elvina. In this charge they lost Major Napier, who was wounded and made prisoner. Major Stanhope was mortally wounded. Sir John was at the head of every charge. Every thing was done under his own eye. 'Remember Egypt!' said he; and the 42nd drove all before them, as the gallant 50th had done. The Guards were ordered to there support. Their ammunition being all spent, through some mistake, they were falling back: 'Ammunition is coming, you have your bayonets,' said Sir John. This was enough; onwards they rushed, overturning every thing. The enemy kept up their hottest fire upon the spot where they were. It was at this moment Sir John received his death-wound. He was borne off the field by six soldiers of the 42nd, and the Guards. We now advanced to the support of the right, led by Lord Paget. Colonel Beckwith, with the Rifle corps, pushed all before him, and nearly took one of their cannon; but a very superior column forced him to retire. Lord Paget, however, repulsed this column, and dispersed every thing before him; when, the left wing of the French being quite exposed, they withdrew and attacked our

61

centre, under Mannington and Leith; but this position being good, they were easily repulsed. They likewise failed in every attempt on our left. A body of them had got possession of a village on the road to Betanzos, and continued to fire, under cover of it, till dislodged by Lieutenant-colonel Nicholls. Shortly after this, night put a period to the battle of Corunna.

At ten o'clock, General Hope ordered the army to march off the field by brigades, leaving strong picquets to guard the embarkation. I remained in the rear-guard, commanded by Major-General Beresford,[10] occupying the lines in front of Corunna. We had made great fires, and a few of the freshest of our men were left to keep them up, and run round them, to deceive the enemy.

At dawn there was little to embark, save the rear-guard and the reserve, commanded by Major-General Hill, who had occupied a promontory behind Corunna. We were scarcely arrived on the beach, ere the French began to fire upon the transports in the harbour, from the heights of St Lucia. Then all became a scene of confusion. Several of the masters of the transports cut their cables. Four of the transports ran ashore. Not having time to get them off, we were forced to burn them. The ships of war soon silenced the French guns, and we saw no more of them. There was no regularity in our taking the boats. The transport that I got to, had part of seven regiments on board.

The Spaniards are a courageous people: the women waved their handkerchiefs to us from the rocks, whilst the men manned the batteries against the French, to cover our embarkation. Unmindful of themselves, they braved a superior enemy, to assist a friend who was unable to afford them further relief, whom they had no prospect of ever seeing again.

Secure within the wooden walls, bad as our condition was, I felt comparatively happy in being so fortunate as to be on board the same vessel with Donald. In relieving his wants, I felt less my own, and was less teased by the wit and ribaldry of my fellow-sufferers; who, now that they were regularly served with provisions, and exempt from the fatigues of marching and the miseries of cold, were as happy, in their rags and full bellies, as any men in England.

For two days after we came on board, I felt the most severe pains through my whole body: the change was so great, from the extreme cold of the winter nights, which we had passed almost without covering, to the suffocating heat of a crowded transport. This was not the most disagreeable part: vermin began to abound. We had not been without them in our march: but now we had dozens for one we had then. In vain we killed them; they appeared to increase from the ragged and dirty clothes, of which we had no means of freeing ourselves. Complaint was vain. Many were worse than myself: I had escaped without a wound; and, thank God! though I had not a shirt upon my back, I had my health, after the two first days, as well as ever I had it.

On the morning of the tenth day after our embarkation, I was condoling with Donald, who was now quite blind. 'I will never be a soldier again, O Thomas! I will be nothing but Donald the blind man. Had I been killed, – if you had left me to die in Spain – it would have been far better to have lain still in a wreath of now [sic], than be, all my life, a blind beggar, a burden on my friends. Oh! if it would please God to take my life from me!' – 'Land a head! Old England once again!' was called from mouth to mouth. Donald burst into tears: 'I shall never see Scotland again; it is me that is the poor dark man!' A hundred ideas rushed upon my mind, and overcame me. Donald clasped me to his breast; – our tears flowed uninterrupted.

We anchored that same day at Plymouth, but were not allowed to land. Our Colonel kept us on board until we got new clothing. Upon our landing, the people came round us, showing all manner of kindness, carrying the lame and leading the blind. We were received into every house as if we had been their own relations. How proud did I feel to belong to such a people![11]

We were marched to Ashford barracks, in the county of Kent, where we remained from the month of February, 1809, until we were marched to Gosport camp, where the army was forming for a secret expedition. During the five weeks we lay in camp, Donald joined us in good health and spirits. All the time I lay at Ashford, I had letters regularly from my mother, which whiled away the time.

We sailed from the Downs on the 28th of July, and reached Flushing in thirty hours, where we landed without opposition. Our regiment was the first that disembarked. We were brigaded, along within the 68th and 85th regiments, under the command of Major-General De Rottenburg.[12] Here, again, as in South America, I was forced to work in the trenches, in forming the batteries against Flushing.

On the night of the 7th of August, the French sallied out upon our works, but were quickly forced back, with great loss. They were so drunk, many of them, that they could not defend themselves; neither could they run away: we, in fact, gave up the pursuit; our hearts would not allow us to kill such helpless wretches, a number of whom could not even ask for mercy.

On the evening of the 10th, we had a dreadful storm of thunder and rain. At the same time, the French Governor opened the sluices, and broke down the sea-dikes, when the water poured in upon us, and we were forced to leave the trenches. However, on the 13th, in the evening, we commenced a dreadful fire upon the town, from the batteries, and vessels in the harbour, which threw bombs and rockets on one side, whilst the batteries plyed them with round shot on the other. I was stunned and bewildered by the noise; the bursting of bombs and falling of chimneys, all adding to the incessant roar of the artillery. The smoke of the burning houses and guns, formed altogether a scene not to be remembered but with horror, which was increased, at every cessation from firing (which was very short), by the piercing shrieks of the inhabitants, the wailings of distress, and howling of dogs. The impression was such as can never be effaced. After night fell, the firing ceased, save from the mortar batteries. The noise was not so dreadful: the eye was now the sense that conveyed horror to the mind. The enemy had set fire to Old Flushing, whilst the New Town was kept burning by the shells and rockets. The dark flare of the burning, the reflection on the water and sky, made all the space, as far as the eye could reach, appear an abyss of fire. The faint tracts of the bombs, and luminous train of the rockets, darting towards, and falling into the flames, conveyed an idea to my mind so appalling, that I turned away and shuddered.

This night, our regiment was advanced a good way in front, upon a sea-dike, through which the enemy had made a cut, to let the water in upon our works. Towards midnight, when the tide was ebb, Colonel Pack[13] made a sally into one of the enemy's batteries. We crossed the cut in silence; Colonel Pack entered first, and struck off the sentinel's head at one blow. We spiked their guns, after a severe brush. At the commencement, as I leaped into the works, an officer seized my firelock before I could recover my balance, and was in the act to cut me down; the sword was descending, when the push of a bayonet forced him to the ground. It was Donald, who fell upon us both. I extricated myself as soon as possible, rose, and fell to work; there was no time to congratulate. The enemy had commenced a heavy fire upon us, and we were forced to retire with forty prisoners. We lost a great number of men killed, wounded, and missing. Donald was amongst the latter, but joined in the morning.

Next morning, Monnet surrendered, and we marched into Flushing, scarce a house of which had escaped; all was a scene of death and desolation.

The wet and fatigue of the last few days had made me ill. I was scarce able to stand, yet I did not report myself sick. I thought it would wear off. Next night I was upon guard. The night was clear and chill; a thin white vapour seemed to extend around as far as I could see; the only parts free from it were the sand heights. It covered the low place where we lay, and was such as you see early in the morning, before the sun is risen, but more dense. I felt very uncomfortable in it; my two hours I thought never would expire; I could not breathe with freedom. Next morning I was in a burning fever, at times; at other times, trembling and chilled with cold: I was unfit to rise, or walk upon my feet. The surgeon told me, I had taken the country disorder, I was sent to the hospital; my disease was the same as that of which hundreds were dying. My spirits never left me; a ray of hope would break in upon me, the moment I got ease, between the attacks of this most severe malady.

I was sent, with many others, to Braeburnlees,[14] where I remained eight weeks ill – very ill indeed. All the time I was in the hospital, my soul was oppressed by the distresses of my fellow-sufferers, and shocked at the conduct of the hospital men. Often have I seen them fighting over the expiring bodies of the patients, their eyes not yet closed in death, for articles of apparel that two had seized at once: cursing and oaths mingling with the dying groans and prayers of the poor sufferers. How dreadful to think, as they were carried from each side of me, it might be my turn next! There was none to comfort, none to give a drink of water, with a pleasant countenance. I had now time to reflect with bitterness on my past conduct; here I learned the value of a parent's kindness.

I had been unable to write since my illness, and I longed to tell my mother where I was, that I might hear from her. I crawled along the wall of the hospital to the door, to see if I could find one more convalescent than myself, to bring me paper. I could not trust the hospital men with the money. To see the face of heaven, and breathe the pure air, was a great inducement to this difficult exertion.

I feebly, and with anxious joy, pushed up the door! horrid moment, dreadful sight! Donald lay upon the barrow, at the stair-head, to be carried to the dead-room; his face was uncovered, and part of his body naked. The light forsook my eyes, I became dreadfully sick, and fell upon the body. When I recovered again, there was a vacancy of thought, and incoherence of ideas, that remained with me for some time; and it was long before I could open a door without feeling an unpleasant sensation.

When I became convalescent, I soon recovered my wonted health. The regiment arrived at Braeburnless upon Christmas day; and I commenced my duties as a soldier. By the death of Donald, I had again, become a solitary individual; nor did I again form a friendship, while we lay here, which was until May 1810; at which time we got the route for Deal. We remained there until the month of September, when an order came for a draught of 600 men, for service in Portugal; of which number I was one.

Up until this point, the narrative by 'Thomas' is straightforward and internally consistent, albeit the account of the battle of Corunna has obviously been lifted (probably by John Howell) from another history. The story of the retreat which preceded it on the other hand does appear to be an eyewitness description and it should therefore be noted that while James Todd, the supposed author according to Howell's inscription, afterwards gained bars to his Military General Service (MGS) medal for Rolieia and Vimeiro, he was left behind in Lisbon and did not take part in the Corunna campaign. When Moore bravely marched into Spain he left a surprising number of men behind in Portugal. Some of them were simply stragglers, while others more legitimately were sick in hospital or were employed in various rear-party jobs. There were so many of them in fact that when Sir Arthur Wellesley returned to resume command in Portugal some months later he was able to form two battalions of detachments from these men, which fought under him at Talavera on 28 July 1809. One of the men, serving in the 2nd Battalion of Detachments was James Todd, and so too was William Farquhar. As discussed earlier the latter would at first sight appear the likeliest candidate for Thomas' friend Donald MacDonald, but the rolls clearly show that Farquhar served neither at Corunna nor at Walcheren.

Four of the August 1806 draft, David Faulds, James Moody, David Walker and Peter Yellet, would be returned as killed in action or otherwise dead, but none died at Walcheren or at any time shortly afterwards – in short the Donald MacDonald described in the narrative never existed. That is not to say that Thomas did not find one of his comrades laid out as described, but if so that man had not gone to South America with him.

Be that as it may, with Farquhar still in Spain the original ten candidates are thus reduced to five. Of those, Joseph Shuder, also known as Johannes Shyder, deserted on 28 July 1809, the very day the regiment sailed for Walcheren. Another, Edward Floyd, eventually survived to claim the Military General Service medal for all of the battles described by Thomas, but he was an Irishman from Londonderry, not a young Scots lad from Edinburgh. Similarly William Mackee was not only Irish enough to claim his MGS as a Kilmainham pensioner, but unlike Thomas he came through the Walcheren campaign unscathed only to be badly wounded at Waterloo and was in hospital at Brussels from June 1815 until at least the end of the year. Of the two remaining men, another Irishman, Joseph Mulholland[15] can also be eliminated, for according to the regiment's quarterly muster rolls he qualified for additional pay in May 1808, indicating that far from being a fresh-faced young recruit, he had originally enlisted as long ago as 1801 when Thomas was just 10 years old.

Thus, by an inexorable process of elimination we are left only with Joseph Sinclair, which is not to say, given the unhappy circumstances of his enlistment, that his real name may not have been Thomas after all. Significantly enough, not only did Joseph Sinclair go out with that draft to South America and come through the Corunna campaign, but the muster roll also records him as returning from Walcheren on board a hospital ship in December 1809, which means that up until this point in the story the experiences of Joseph Sinclair and the Thomas of the *Journal* correspond exactly – and uniquely.

Afterwards it is a different matter and, as we shall see, the second half of the narrative must owe rather more to Todd and Gavin.

3

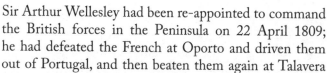

Sir Arthur Wellesley had been re-appointed to command the British forces in the Peninsula on 22 April 1809; he had defeated the French at Oporto and driven them out of Portugal, and then beaten them again at Talavera on 29 July. However, exploitation of the victory was frustrated by supply failures and lack of co-operation from the Spanish authorities, with the result that a strong French offensive in the late summer of 1810 saw a retreat back into Portugal, and it was at this point that the 71st returned to the Peninsula.

Since it last served there the regiment had undergone something of a transformation. By all accounts the 71st were a pretty sorry sight when they disembarked from captivity in Argentina; and it is not entirely certain whether, having been stationed in South Africa, they actually went across to Argentina in their kilts, but they certainly needed new ones when they came home. However, their commanding officer, 'Sweet' Dennis Pack advised the adjutant general's office that he intended to cloth the men in tartan trousers as these could be run up more quickly than kilts. This was duly approved and a contemporary sketch by Atkinson does indeed depict them fighting at Vimeiro in feather bonnets and tartan trews. The transformation, however, did not end there, for in early 1809, prior to going to Walcheren, the regiment was re-trained as a light infantry unit and in the process lost its tartan trousers in favour of plain ones and saw its bonnets dramatically altered in appearance.

In its original form the Kilmarnock bonnet worn by all Highland soldiers at this time was a drum-shaped article knitted from dark blue wool and usually sporting a red and white chequered band around the bottom half. This was then adorned with a spray of black ostrich feathers, which looked well on parade but tended to vanish on active service. On their conversion into light infantry the 71st dispensed with the feathers and probably through the insertion of a cardboard stiffening, stretched the bonnet upwards to mirror the shape of the regulation military cap or chaco. It was still a bonnet, however, and as we shall see Thomas very properly still referred to it as such in his narrative.

SAILS for the Peninsula – Description of Lisbon – Joins the army at Sobral – Actions at Sobral – Retires behind the British lines – Retreat of the French to Santarem – Their atrocities on the way – Mortifying discovery in a wine store – Retreat of the French to the Aguida.

There were six companies, of 100 men each, embarked in two frigates; 300 in each. I was on board the Melpomene.

During the six days' sail to Lisbon my thoughts were not the most agreeable. I was on my way to that country in which I had already suffered so much. My health was good, but my spirits were very low; I could not yet bring myself to associate with the other men, so as to feel pleasure in their amusements. I found it necessary to humour them in many things, and be obliging to all. I was still called saucy, and little courted by my comrades to join them. I had changed my bedfellow more than once; they not liking my dry manner, as they called it.

On the seventh day after leaving Deal, we were landed at Blackhorse Square, Lisbon, amidst the shouts of the inhabitants. We were marched to the top of the town, and billeted in a convent. A good many were billeted in the town, the convent being not large enough to contain us. I was billeted upon a cook-shop.

Two years before, while encamped before Lisbon, I had often wished to enter the town; now, I as ardently wished to leave it. I was sickened every hour of the day with the smell of garlic and oil. Every thing there is fried in oil that will fry: Oil and garlic is their universal relish. Cleanliness they have not the least conception of. The town is a dunghill from end to end; their principal squares are not even free from heaps of filth. You may make a shift to walk by the side of the streets, with clean shoes; but cross one, if you dare. I inquired at one of our regiment, who had been left sick, if they had any scavengers? 'Yes,' said he, 'they have one.' 'He will have a great many under him?' 'None.' 'What folly to have only one to such a city!' 'And that one, only when he may please to come.' 'You joke with me.' 'No, I don't: The rain is their street-cleaner; he will be here soon; there will be clean streets while he remains; then, they prepare work for him again.'

To my great joy, we paraded in the grand square, on the seventh day after our arrival, and marched in sections, to the music of our bugles, to join the army; having got our camp equipments, consisting of a camp-kettle and bill-hook, to every six men; a blanket, a canteen, and haversack, to each man. Orders had been given, that each soldier, on his march, should carry along with him three days' provision. Our mess of six cast lots who should be cook the first day, as we were to carry the kettle day about: the lot fell to me. My knapsack contained two shirts, two pair of stockings, one pair overalls, two shoe-brushes, a shaving box, one pair spare shoes, and a few other articles; my great coat and blanket above the knapsack; my canteen with water was slung over my shoulder, on one side; my haversack, with beef and bread, on the other; sixty round of ball-cartridge, and the camp-kettle above all.

I was now well broke down by what I had been in my first campaign with Moore. How different was Tom, marching to school with his satchel on his back, from Tom, with his musket and kitt; a private soldier, an atom of an army, unheeded by all; his comforts sacrificed to ambition, his untimely death talked of with indifference, and only counted in the gross with hundreds, without a sigh!

We halted, on the first night, at a palace belonging to the Queen of Portugal, called Safrea, where we were joined by the Honourable Henry Cadogan, our Colonel.[1] Next day, the 14th October 1810, we joined the army at Sobral de Monte Agraco, a small town surrounded by hills. On the front is a hill, called by our men *Windmill Hill*, from a number of windmills which were upon it; in the rear, another they called *Gallows Hill*, from a gibbet standing there.

We had not been three hours in the town, and were busy cooking, when the alarm sounded. There were nine British, and three Portuguese regiments in the town. We were all drawn up, and remained under arms; expecting, every moment, to receive the enemy, whose skirmishers covered Windmill Hill. In about an hour the light companies of all the regiments were ordered out, alongst with the 71st. Colonel Cadogan called to us, at the foot of the hill, 'My lads, this is the first affair I have ever been in with you; show me what you can do, now or never.' We gave a hurra, and advanced up the hill, driving their advanced skirmishers before us, until about half-way up, when we commenced a heavy fire, and were as hotly received. In the meantime the remaining regiments evacuated the town. The enemy pressed so hard upon us, we were forced to make the best of our way down the hill, and were closely followed by the French, through the town, up Gallows Hill. We got behind a mud wall, and kept our ground in spite of their utmost efforts. Here we lay upon our arms all night.

Next morning, by day-break, there was not a Frenchman to be seen. As soon as the sun was fairly up, we advanced into the town, and began a search for provisions, which were now become very scarce; and, to our great joy, found a large storehouse full of dry fish, flour, rice, and sugar, besides bales of cloth. All now became bustle and mirth; fires were kindled, and every man became a cook. Scones were the order of the day. Neither flour nor sugar were wanting, and the water was plenty; so I fell to bake myself a flour scone. Mine was mixed and laid upon the fire, and I, hungry enough, watching it. Though neither neat nor comely, I was anticipating the moment when it would be eatable. Scarce was it warm, ere the bugle sounded to arms. Then was the joy that reigned a moment before, turned to execrations. I snatched my scone off the fire, raw as it was, put it into my haversack, and formed. We remained under arms until dark; and then took up our old quarters upon Gallows Hill, where I ate my raw scone, sweetly seasoned by hunger. In our advance to the town, we were much entertained by some of our men who had got over a wall, the day before, when the enemy were in the rear; and, now, were put to their shifts to get over again, and scarce could make it out.

Next morning, the French advanced to a mud wall, about forty yards in front of the one we lay behind. It rained heavily this day, and there was very little firing. During the night we received orders to cover the bugle and tartans of our bonnets with black crape, which had been served out to us during the day, and to put on our great-coats. Next morning the French, seeing us thus, thought we had retired, and left the Portuguese to guard the heights. With dreadful shouts, they leaped over that wall before which they had stood, when guarded by British. We were scarce able to withstand their fury. To retreat was impossible; all behind being ploughed land, rendered deep by the rain. There was not a moment to hesitate. To it we fell, pell-mell, French and British mixed together. It was a trial of strength in single combat; every man had his opponent, many had two. I got one up to the wall, on the point of my bayonet. He was unhurt. I would have spared him, but he would not spare himself. He cursed and defied me, nor ceased to attack my life, until he fell, pierced by my bayonet. His breath died away in a curse and menace. This was the work of a moment: I was compelled to this extremity. I was again attacked, but my antagonist fell, pierced by a random shot. We soon forced them to retire over the wall, cursing their mistake. At this moment, I stood gasping for breath; not a shoe on my feet: my bonnet had fallen to the ground. Unmindful of my situation, I followed the enemy over the wall. We pursued them about a mile, and then fell back to the scene of our struggle. It was covered with dead and wounded, bonnets and shoes trampled and stuck in the mud I recovered a pair of shoes: whether they had been mine or not, I cannot tell; they were good.

Here I first got any plunder. A French soldier lay upon the ground dead. He had fallen backwards; his hat had fallen off his head, which was kept up by his knapsack. I struck the hat with my foot, and felt it rattle; seized it in a moment, and, in the lining, found a gold watch and silver crucifix. I kept them, as I had as good a right to them as any other. Yet they were not valuable in my estimation. At this time, life was held by so uncertain a tenure, and my comforts were so scanty, that I would have given the watch for a good meal and a dry shirt. There was not a dry stitch on my back at the time, nor for the next two days.

In a short time the French sent in a flag of truce, for leave to carry off their wounded, which was granted. They advanced to their old ground, and we lay looking at each other for three days; the two first of which the rain never ceased to pour; the third day was good and dry. During this time, the French withdrew their lines, and left only picquets.

On the third day, an officer and twelve men went to the wall, as the French sentinels were become very remiss. He looked over, and saw a picquet of fifty men, playing cards, and amusing themselves. Our party levelled their muskets, and gave them a volley. They took to their heels, officers and all. There was no further attack made that day; and we retired behind the line of batteries, at night, quite worn out with hunger and fatigue.

For five nights I had never been in bed, and, during good part of that time, it had rained hard. We were upon ploughed land, which was rendered so soft, that we sunk over the shoes at every step. The manner in which I passed the night was thus: I placed my canteen upon the ground, put my knapsack above, and sat upon it, supporting my head upon my hands; my musket, between my knees, resting upon my shoulder, and my blanket over all, – ready to start, in a moment, at the least alarm. The nights were chill: indeed, in the morning, I was so stiff, I could not stand or move with ease for some time; my legs were benumbed to the knees. I was completely wet three nights out of the five. A great number of the men took the fever and ague, after we retired behind the lines. I was not a whit the worse.

On our arrival behind the lines, our brigade, consisting of the 50th, 71st, and 92nd,[2] commanded by Major-General Sir William Erskine,[3] was quartered in a small village, called Sabreira. Our first care was to place out-posts and sentinels between the batteries, about twenty yards distant from each other. We communicated with the foot guards on our right,[4] and the Brunswick infantry on our left.[5] Those off duty were employed throwing up batteries and breast-works, or breaking up the roads. The day after we fell into the lines, the French placed sentinels in front of us, without any dispute. There was a small valley and stream of water between us.

We remained thus for five weeks; every day, when off duty, forming defensive works, or breaking up the roads; it being a place that no army could pass, save upon the highway. The advanced picquet of the French lay in a windmill; ours, consisting of one captain, two subalterns, and 400 men, in a small village. There was only a distance of about 150 yards between us. We learned from the deserters, that the French were much in want of provisions. To provoke them, our sentinels, at times, would fix a biscuit to the point of their bayonets, and present to them. One day the French had a bullock, in endeavouring to kill which, the butcher missed his blow, and the animal ran off right into our lines. The French looked so foolish, we hurrahed at them, secured the bullock, brought him in front, killed him in style. They looked on, but dared not approach to seize him. Shortly after, an officer and four men came with a flag of truce, and supplicated in the most humble manner for the half of the bullock, which they got for godsake.

On the evening of the 14th November, the French made their outposts stronger than they had yet been, and kindled great fires after dark. We were all under arms an hour before day, expecting to be attacked; but, when the day dawned, there was not a Frenchman to be seen. As soon as the sun was up, we set off after them.

When we arrived at Sobral, we found a great number of our men, who had been wounded on the 14th and

15th October, besides a greater proportion of French wounded and sick. We were told by our men, that the weakly men, and the baggage of the French army, had been sent off eight days before. We were halted at Sobral, until provisions came up; when three days' allowance was served out to each man. We again commenced our advance. The weather was very bad; it rained for a great part of the time without intermission. On the fourth day, we took about 100 prisoners, who had concealed themselves in a wood.

This retreat brought to my mind the Corunna race. We could not advance one hundred yards, without seeing dead soldiers of the enemy stretched upon the road, or at a little distance from it, who had lain down to die, unable to proceed through hunger and fatigue. We could not pity them, miserable as they were. Their retreat resembled more that of famished wolves than men. Murder and devastation marked their way; every house was a sepulchre, a cabin of horrors! Our soldiers used to wonder why the Frenchmen were not swept by heaven from the earth, when they witnessed their cruelties. In a small town called Safrea, I saw twelve dead bodies lying in one house upon the floor! – Every house contained traces of their wanton barbarity. Often has a shade of doubt crossed my mind, when reading the accounts of former atrocities; often would I think – they are exaggerated. Thank God we live in more civilized times. How dreadfully were my doubts removed! I cease to describe, lest I raise doubts similar to my own.

At this time, I got a distaste I could never overcome. A few of us went into a wine-store, where there was a large tun, with a ladder to get to the top, in which was a hole about two feet square. There was not much wine in it, so we buckled our canteen straps together, until a camp-kettle attached to them reached the liquor. We drew it up once – we all drank: down it went again – it got entangled with something at the bottom of the tun – a candle was lowered; – to our great disappointment, the corpse of a French soldier lay upon the bottom. Sickness came upon me; and, for a long time afterwards, I shuddered at the sight of red wine. The Portuguese soldiers never would drink red wine, if white could be got. When I asked the reason, their reply was, they knew how it was made.

We continued our pursuit, every day taking more or less prisoners, who were unable to keep up with the main army, until we came in front of Santarem. Here we piled arms upon the sandy ground; the French were in possession of the heights. Colonel Cadogan made the smartest of the men run races, in front, for fun. From this sport, we were suddenly called to form line for attack: but the French position was too strong for us. By this time it was quite dark, and we had a large plain to cross, to a village where we were to halt all night. In our march we were put into confusion, and a good number of the men knocked over, by a flock of goats, of which we caught a few, which made a delicious supper for us. On our arrival at the village we were forced to break up the doors, as the inhabitants would not let us in.

Next morning was very wet. The following evening, we halted at a village but two Portuguese regiments had been before us, and swept all away. We sent out parties to forage, and got some Indian corn, which we ground ourselves, at a mill, the inhabitants having all fled. We were then quartered in a convent in Alcanterina, where we lay from the beginning of December until 5th March 1811. Provisions were very scarce. Fatigue parties were sent out every day, for Indian corn and pot-herbs. We had beef; but we could not subsist upon beef alone, which was seldom good, being far driven, very tough, and lean. An accident procured us a short relief. Some of our men, amusing themselves in piercing the ceiling with their bayonets, discovered a trap-door, and found a great concealed store of food and valuables. We fared well while it lasted. Having very little duty, our time was spent at football. We were very badly off for shoes; but, by good luck, discovered a quantity of leather in a tan-yard. Those who found it, helped themselves first, and were wasting it. The Colonel then ordered each man a pair of soles and heels, to be put up in his knapsack.

The French gave us the slip, at the commencement of their retreat, by placing wooden guns in their batteries, and stuffing old clothes with straw, which they put in place of their sentinels. By this means, their retreat was not discovered for two days; and, only then, by one of our cavalry riding up to their lines to take a sentinel prisoner, who appeared asleep. As soon as it was ascertained there was a trick, we set off after them: and, beginning to come up with them, took a good many prisoners. Our advance was so rapid, that provisions could not be brought up to us. We were often two days without bread. The rear of the army being always served first, we, who were in advance, seldom got enough. For four or five days, we were so close up with the French, that we had skirmishes with them every day; but, having received no bread for three days, we were forced to halt for two, until we got a supply. During these two days, I had an opportunity of witnessing the desolation caused by the French soldiers. In one small village, I counted seventeen dead bodies of men, women, and children; and most of the houses were burnt to the ground.

The Portuguese were not un-revenged of their destroyers; great numbers of whom had lain down, unable to proceed, from wounds or fatigue, and had been either killed by the peasantry, or died, unheard, amongst the devastation themselves or their fellows had made.

At this time, we were forced either to forage or starve, as we were far in advance of our supplies. I was now as much a soldier as any of my comrades, when it fell to my turn. At this time I was so fortunate as to procure the full of my haversack of Indian corn heads, which we used to call turkeys. I was welcomed with joy. We rubbed out some of our corn, and boiled it with a piece of beef; roasted some of our turkeys, and were happy. Bread at length coming up, we received three days' allowance a man, and recommenced our advance; but never came up with the enemy until they reached the Aguida, on the 9th April 1811.

We were marched into winter quarters. Our division, the 2nd, was posted in a small town called Alberguira, on the frontiers of Spain, where we remained till the 30th April.[6] During our stay, I had an adventure of a disagreeable kind. I was strolling, as usual, when I heard a voice pleading, in the most earnest manner, in great distress. I hastened to the spot, and found a Portuguese muleteer taking a bundle from a girl. I ran up to him and bade him desist: he flew into a passion, drew his knife, and made a stab at me. I knocked him down with my fist; the girl screamed and wept. I stood on my guard, and bade him throw away his knife. He rose, his eyes glistening with rage, and stabbed furiously at me. In vain I called to him: I drew my bayonet. I had no choice; yet, unwilling to kill, I held it by the point, and knocked him to the ground with the hilt, as he rushed to close with me; left him there, and brought home the weeping girl to her parents.

— ♦ —

BATTLE of Fuentes d'Onoro – Contrast between the French and British soldiers when advancing to charge – Distressing march to Albuera – Pursuit of General Girard – Surprise and total rout of his army.

On the 30th of April, we set off for Fuentes d'Onoro, where we arrived, after a fatiguing march of three days; and formed line, about two miles in rear of the town, hungry and weary, having had no bread for the last two days.

On the 3rd of May at day-break, all the cavalry, and sixteen light companies, occupied the town. We stood under arms until three o'clock, when a staff-officer rode up to our Colonel, and gave orders for our advance. Colonel Cadogan put himself at our head, saying 'My lads, you have had no provision these two days; there is plenty in the hollow in front, let us down and divide it.' We advanced as quick as we could run, and met the light companies retreating as fast as they could. We continued to advance, at double-quick time, our firelocks at the trail, our bonnets in our hands. They called to us, 'Seventy-first, you will come back quicker than you advance.' We soon came full in front of the enemy. The Colonel cried, 'Here is food, my lads, cut away.' Thrice we waved our bonnets, and thrice we cheered; brought our firelocks to the charge, and forced them back through the town.

How different the duty of the French officers from ours! They, stimulating the men by their example; the men vociferating, each chafing each until they appear in a fury, shouting, to the points of our bayonets. After the first huzza, the British officers, restraining their men, still as death – 'Steady, lads, steady.' is all you hear; and that in an under tone.

The French had lost a great number of men in the streets. We pursued them about a mile out of the town, trampling over the dead and wounded; but their cavalry bore down upon us, and forced us back into the town, where we kept our ground, in spite of their utmost efforts.

In this affair, my life was most wonderfully preserved. In forcing the French through the town, during our first advance, a bayonet went through between my side and clothes, to my knapsack, which stopped its progress. The Frenchman to whom the bayonet belonged, fell, pierced by a musket-ball from my rear-rank man. Whilst freeing myself from the bayonet, a ball took off part of my right-shoulder wing, and killed my rear-rank man, who fell upon me. Narrow as this escape was, I felt no uneasiness, I was become so inured to danger and fatigue.

During this day, the loss of men was great. In our retreat back to the town, when we halted to check the enemy, who bore hard upon us, in their attempts to break our line, often was I obliged to stand with a foot upon each side of a wounded man, who rung my soul with prayers I could not answer, and pierced my heart with his cries to be lifted out of the way of the cavalry. While my heart bled for them, I have shaken them rudely off.

We kept up our fire, until long after dark. About one o'clock in the morning, we got four ounces of bread served out to each man, which had been collected out of the haversacks of the Foot Guards. After the firing had ceased, we began to search through the town, and found plenty of flour, bacon, and sausages, on which we feasted heartily, and lay down on our blankets, wearied to death. My shoulder was as black as a coal, from the recoil of my musket; for this day I had fired 107 rounds of ball-cartridge. Sore as I was, I slept as sound as a top, till I was awakened by the loud call of the bugle, an hour before day.

Soon as it was light, the firing commenced, and was kept up until about ten o'clock, when Lieutenant Stewart, of our regiment, was sent with a flag of truce, for leave to carry off our wounded from the enemy's lines, which was granted; and at the same time, they carried off theirs from ours. As soon as the wounded were all got in, many of whom had lain bleeding all night – many both a day and a night – the French brought down a number of bands of music to a level piece of ground, about ninety or a hundred yards broad, that lay between us. They continued to play until sunset; whilst the men were dancing, and diverting themselves at football. We were busy cooking the remainder of our sausages, bacon, and flour.

After dark, a deserter from the French told us that there were five regiments of grenadiers picked out to storm the town. In the French army, the grenadiers are all in regiments by themselves. We lay down, fully accoutred, as usual, and slept in our blankets. An hour before day, we were ready to receive the enemy.

About half-past nine o'clock, a great gun from the French line, which was answered by one from ours, was the signal to engage. Down they came, shouting as usual. We kept them at bay, in spite of their cries and formidable looks. How different their appearance from ours; their hats set round with feathers, their beards long and black, gave them a fierce look. Their stature was superior to ours; most of us were young. We looked like boys they like savages. But we had the true spirit in us. We foiled them, in every attempt to take the town, until about eleven o'clock, when we were overpowered, and forced through the streets, contesting every inch.

A French dragoon, who was dealing death around, forced his way up to near where I stood. Every moment I expected to be cut down. My piece was empty; there was not a moment to lose. I got a stab at him, beneath the ribs, upwards; he gave a back stroke, before he fell, and cut the stock of my musket in two; thus I stood unarmed. I soon got another, and fell to work again.

During the preceding night, we had been reinforced by the 79th regiment, Colonel Cameron commanding, who was killed about this time.[7] Notwithstanding all our efforts, the enemy forced us out of the town, then halted, and formed close column betwixt us and it. While they stood thus, the havoc amongst them was dreadful. Gap after gap was made by our cannon, and as quickly filled up. Our loss was not so severe, as we stood in open files. While we stood thus, firing at each other as quick as we could, the 88th regiment advanced from the lines, charged the enemy, and forced them to give way. As we passed over the ground where they had stood, it lay two and three deep of dead and wounded. While we drove them before us through the town, in turn, they were reinforced, which only served to increase the slaughter. We forced them out, and kept possession all day.

After sunset, the enemy sent in a flag of truce, for leave to carry off their wounded and bury their dead; which was granted. About ten o'clock, we were relieved, and retired back to our lines. In these affairs we lost four officers, and two taken prisoners, besides 400 men killed and wounded. This statement, more than any words of mine, will give an idea of the action at Fuentes d'Onoro.[8]

On my arrival in the lines, when unpacking my knapsack, I found a ball had pierced into the centre of it, and dimpled the back of my shoe-brush. We remained seven days in the lines, the French showing themselves three or four times a day. On the 7th they retired; and we went back to our old quarters in Alberguira.

While here, we received a draught of 200 men, and again set off. Our division consisted of the 24th, 42nd, 50th, 71st, 79th, 92nd, and one battalion of the King's German Legion.[9] We were assembled after dark, and marched off, all that night, next day, and night following, when we arrived at a town, situated upon a hill, called Pennemacore. The heat was so great, we were unable to keep together. I do not believe that ten men of a company marched into the town together; they had lain down upon the road, or straggled behind, unable to climb the hill. Two men belonging to the Foot Guards and one of the 50th, fell down dead, from heat and thirst. Two or three times, my sight grew dim; my mouth was dry as dust; my lips one continued blister. I had water in my canteen, but it tasted bitter as soot, and it was so warm it made me sick. At this time, I first tried a thing which gave me a little relief: I put a small pebble into my mouth, and sucked it. This I always did afterwards, in similar situations, and found drought easier to be borne.

Early next morning, the 50th, 71st, and 92nd, were marched on; and the remainder of the division returned to their old quarters at Alberguira. After a most distressing march of seven days, we arrived at Badajoz, where we remained one night; then marched nine miles, to a town called Talavera Real, where we halted three days; then marched, at six o'clock in the evening, to the camp at Albuera, a few days after the battle, which had been the cause of our rapid movement.[10] We remained in camp at Albuera a short time; then marched to Elvas, a strong town on the Portuguese frontier, opposite Badajos. We remained here four days; and then marched into camp, at Toro de Moro, where we remained for a considerable time.

Here I enjoyed the beauties of the country more than at any former period. Often when off duty, have I wandered into the woods to enjoy the cool refreshing shade of the cork-trees, and breathe the richly perfumed air, loaded with the fragrance of innumerable aromatic plants. One evening as I lay in the wood, thinking upon home, sweeter than all the surrounding sweets, almost overcome by my sensations, I heard, at a small distance, music. I listened some time ere I could be satisfied it was so. It ceased all at once; then began sweeter than before. I arose, and approached nearer, to avoid the noise of a small burn that ran rippling near where I had been reclining. I soon knew the air; I crept nearer, and could distinguish the words; I became rivetted to the spot: that moment compensated for all I had suffered in Spain. I felt that pleasure which softens the heart, and overflows at the eyes. The words that first struck my ear were, 'Why did I leave my Jeanie, my daddy's cot, an' a', To wander from my country, sweet Caledonia.'

Soon as the voice ceased, I looked through the underwood, and saw four or five soldiers seated on the turf, who sung in their turn, Scotland's sweetest songs of remembrance. When they retired, I felt as if I was bereft of all enjoyment. I slowly retired to the camp, to reflect and spend a sleepless night. Every opportunity, I returned to the scene of my happiness; and had the pleasure, more than once to enjoy this company unseen.

While encamped here, we received a draft of 350 men from England. Shortly after, we marched to Burbo, to protect the siege of Badajos. We lay here till the 17th June, when Soult raised the siege, and we retired to Portalegre. We then were marched to Castello de Vido, another hill town, about two leagues from Portalegre.

There is now an abrupt and unexplained gap of some four months in the narrative. Significantly the 71st muster rolls reveal that just at this time Joseph Sinclair, the original author of the narrative, was consigned as sick, first to the general hospital at Abrantes and then to the one at Lisbon.[11] It was most likely a recurrence of the notorious Walcheren Fever (malaria) which afflicted so many veterans of that campaign and he was still in hospital when the narrative resumes with the raid on Arroyo dos Molinos in late October 1811. It is must be at this point therefore that James Todd takes up the story and as we shall see not only do his adventures differ considerably from those of Joseph Sinclair, but notwithstanding John Howell's efforts, the style of the narrative is also different.

On the 22nd October, we received information that General Girard, with 4000 men, infantry and cavalry, was collecting contributions in Estremadura, and had cut off part of our baggage and supplies. We immediately set off from Portalegre, along with the brigade commanded by General Hill,[12] and, after a most fatiguing march, the weather very bad, we arrived at Malpartida. The French were only ten miles distant. By a near cut, on the Merida road, through Alden del Cano, we got close up to them, on the 27th, at Alcuesca, and were drawn up in columns, with great guns ready to receive them. They had heard nothing of our approach. We went into the town. It was now nigh ten o'clock; the enemy were in Arroyo del Molino, only three miles distant. We got half a pound of rice served out to each man, to be cooked immediately. Hunger made little cooking necessary. The officers had orders to keep their men silent. We were placed in the houses; but our wet and heavy accoutrements were on no account to be taken off. At twelve o'clock, we received our allowance of rum; and, shortly after, the sergeants tapped at the doors, calling not above their breath. We turned out, and, at slow time, continued our march.

The whole night was one continued pour of rain. Weary, and wet to the skin, we trudged on, without exchanging a word; nothing breaking the silence of the night, save the howling of the wolves. The tread of the men was drowned by the pattering of the rain. When day at length broke, we were close upon the town. The French posts had been withdrawn into it, but the embers still glowed in their fires. During the whole march, the 71st had been with the cavalry and horse-artillery, as an advanced guard.

General Hill rode up to our Colonel, and ordered him to make us clean out our pans (as the rain had wet all the priming), form square, and retire a short distance, lest the French cavalry had seen us, and should make an attack: however, the drift was so thick, they could not; it blew right in their faces, when they looked our way. The Colonel told us off in three divisions, and gave us orders to charge up three separate streets of the town, and force our way, without halting, to the other side. We shouldered our arms. The General, taking off his hat, said, 'God be with you – quick march.' On reaching the gates, we gave three cheers, and in we went; the inhabitants calling, 'Live the English!' our piper playing 'Hey Johnny Cope;' the French swearing, fighting in confusion, running here and there, some in their shirts, some half accoutred. The streets were crowded with baggage and men ready to march, all now in one heap of confusion. On we drove: our orders were to take no prisoners, and neither to turn to the right nor left, until we reached the other side of the town.

As we advanced, I saw the French general come out of a house, frantic with rage. Never will I forget the grotesque figure he made, as he threw his cocked hat upon the ground, and stamped upon it, gnashing his teeth. When I got the first glance of him, he had many medals on his breast. In a minute, his coat was as bare as a private's.

We formed, under cover of some old walls. A brigade of French stood in view. We got orders to fire: not ten pieces in a company went off, the powder was again so wet with the rain. A brigade of Portuguese artillery came up. We gave the enemy another volley, leaped the wall, formed column, and drove them over the hill; down which they threw all their baggage, before they surrendered. In this affair, we took about 3000 prisoners, 1600 horse, and 6 pieces of artillery, with a great quantity of baggage, &c.

We were again marched back to Portalegre, where the horses were sold and divided amongst the men, according to their rank. I got 2s. 6d.[13] for my share; but I had provided myself a good assortment of necessaries out of the French stores at Molino.

We remained at Portalegre, until the campaign began, in the month of January 1812. We were in advance, covering the operations against Ciudad Rodrigo and Badajoz. We had a most fatiguing spring, marching and counter-marching between Merida and Almandralajo. We were first marched to Merida, but Dombrosky fled with the utmost precipitation. We then marched against Drouet, who was at Almandralajo; but he, likewise, set off for Zafra, leaving his stores and ammunition, to us a welcome gift. The weather was so wet, the very shoes were soaked off our feet; and many were the contrivances we fell upon to keep them on.

Almandralajo is a low swampy place; the worst town I ever was in, in Spain: our men called it Almandralajo Craco, (cursed). Seldom a day passed but we had a skirmish with the enemy at Merida, or Almandralajo.

In the month of March, we got the route for Albuera, where we formed our lines, and were working at the batteries day and night. An alarm was given three different times, and we were marched on to the position; but nothing occurred, and we fell back.

When I first came upon the spot where the battle of Albuera had been fought, I felt very sad; the whole ground was still covered with the wrecks of an army, bonnets, cartridge-boxes, pieces of belts, old clothes, and shoes: the ground in numerous ridges, under which lay many a heap of mouldering bones. It was a melancholy sight; it made us all very dull for a short time.

The whole army receiving orders to advance, we moved in solid columns, cavalry on right and left. The enemy fell back as we advanced. Our brigade was marched up a hill, where we had a beautiful view of the armies, threatening each other, like two thunder clouds charged with death. Shortly after we were marched into the valley; the enemy fired two or three round shot at us, which did no harm. We were encamped, till next day at noon: when we set off, pursuing them for two days, and were then marched back to Almandralajo Craco, where we lay till the beginning of April.

Next we advanced to cover the operations against Badajoz, which surrendered on the 6th, the day of our arrival. Next morning the band played The Downfall of Paris. We remained until May, when we were marched to Almaraz, where the French had two forts which intercepted our supplies, as they commanded the bridge over the Tagus.

— ♦ —

MARCH to Almaraz – Storming of Fort Almaraz – Retreat from Burgos – Skirmishes, &c. at Alba Tormes – Ludicrous incident there.

Our brigade, consisting of the 50th, 71st, and 92nd regiments, set off, and marched all day, until noon. On the second day, our officers got orders that every person in the village of Almaraz should be put to death; there being none but those belonging to the enemy in it. We marched all night, until break of day next morning, when we halted on a height opposite the large fort, just as they fired their morning gun. As the day broke up, they got sight of our arrival, and gave us a shell or two, which did us no harm. We were moved down the hill out of their view. Then we were marched to the height again, where we stood under arms for a short time, until we were ordered to pile arms and take off our packs. We remained thus until twelve o'clock, when we got half an allowance of liquor; oxen were brought up and killed on the spot; each man received two pounds of beef in lieu of bread. We got this for three days.

On the evening of the third day, General Hill ordered our left companies to move down to the valley, to cover his recognisance. When he returned, the officers were called. A scaling-ladder was given to each section of a company of the left wing, with the exception of two companies. We moved down the hill in a dismal manner; it was so dark we could not see three yards before us. The hill was very steep, and we were forced to wade through whins and scramble down rocks, still carrying the ladders. When day-light, on the morning of the 19th, at length showed us to each other, we were scattered all over the foot of the hill like strayed sheep, not more in one place than were held together by a ladder. We halted, formed, and collected the ladders, then moved on. We had a hollow to pass through to get at the battery. The French had cut a part of the brae-face away, and had a gun that swept right through into the hollow. We made a rush past it, to get under the brae on the other side. The French were busy cooking, and preparing to support the other fort, thinking we would attack it first, as we had lain next it.

On our approach, the French sentinel fired and retired. We halted, fixed bayonets, and moved on in double-quick time. We did not receive above four shot from the battery, until we were under the works, and had the ladders placed to the walls. Their intrenchment proved deeper than we expected, which caused us to splice our ladders under the wall; during which time they annoyed us much, by throwing grenades, stones, and logs over it; for we stood with our pieces cocked and presented. As soon as the ladders were spliced, we forced them from the works, and out of the town, at the point of the bayonet, down the hill and over the bridge. They were in such haste, they cut the bridge before all their men had got over, and numbers were either drowned or taken prisoners. One of our men had the honour to be the first to mount the works.

Fort Napoleon fired two or three shot into Fort Almaraz. We took the hint from this circumstance, and turned the guns of Almarez on Fort Napoleon, and forced the enemy to leave it. It being a bridge of boats, two companies were sent, with brooms, to burn and cut it away; but the enemy, being in superior force upon the other side, compelled them to retire, under cover, until reinforced.

We moved forward to the village of Almaraz, and found plenty of provisions, which had been very scarce with us for some days. We filled our haversacks, and burned the town; then encamped close by it, all night, and marched next morning; leaving a company of sappers and miners to blow up the works. We marched back to our old quarters; and continued marching up and down watching the motions of the enemy.

On the night of the 22nd July, when we were in a wood, we received the joyful news of the defeat of Marmont at Salamanca, and got a double allowance of liquor. Colonel Cadogan took the end of a horn, called *a tot*, and drank, 'Success to the British arms.' Some of us had money, and sent to the village for liquor. We made a little treat, in the best manner we could, and passed a joyful night.

We advanced to Aranjuez, where we lay for some time. It is a palace of the King of Spain. The whole country is beautiful; fruit was very plenty, and of all kinds. We were eight days in the Escurial, and continued to watch the motions of the French alongst the Tagus, skirmishing almost every day. Individuals of the 13th and 14th Light

Dragoons, used to engage, in single combat, with the horsemen of the enemy. Often whole squadrons would be brought to engage, by two men beginning.

We remained thus skirmishing till Lord Wellington raised the siege of Burgos; when we fell back to the Iacama (Jarama), in the beginning of November; then on Alba Tormes, where we skirmished two days and two nights. A part of us here were lining a wall; the French in great strength in front. One of our lads having let his hat fall over, when taking cartridges from it, laid his musket against the wall, went over to the enemy's side, and came back again unhurt. At this very time the bottom of my stock was shot off.

The short time we remained at Tormes, we were very ill off for provisions. One of our men, Thomas Caldwell,[14] found a piece of meat, near the hospital, on the face of the brae; he brought it home, and cooked it. A good part of it was eaten, before one of the men, perceiving him, said, 'What is that you are eating?' Tom said, it was meat he had found. The others looked, and knew it to be the fore-arm of a man: the hand was not at it; it was only the part from a little below the elbow, and above the wrist. The man threw it away, but never looked squeamish; he said it was very sweet, and was never a bit the worse.

The French left strong picquets in front, stole down the river, and crossed, hoping to surprise us, and come upon our rear. We immediately blew up the bridge, and retired. Many of our men had to ford the river. We left a Spanish garrison in the fort, and retired to the heights.

There was a mill on the river side, near the bridge, wherein a number of our men were helping themselves to flour, during the time the others were fording. Our Colonel rode down and forced them out, throwing a handful of flour on each man as he passed out of the mill. When we were drawn up on the heights, he rode along the column, looking for the millers, as we called them. At this moment, a hen put her head out of his coat-pocket, and looked first to one side, and then to another. We began to laugh; we could not restrain ourselves. He looked amazed and furious at us, then around. At length the major rode up to him, and requested him to kill the fowl outright, and put it into his pocket. The Colonel, in his turn, laughed, called his servant, and the millers were no more looked after.

We moved along the heights, for two or three miles, towards the main body of the army, and lay down in column for a few minutes, until Lord Wellington came up and reconnoitred the movements of the enemy, when we immediately got orders to follow the line of march. We continued to follow, for some time, until we came to a place covered over with old ammunition-barrels and the wrecks of an army. This was the ground the battle of Salamanca had been fought on. We got not a moment to reflect. The word was given, 'Fix bayonets, throw off all lumber;' and we were moved up the hill at double-quick time. We pushed up as hard as possible, reached the top almost out of breath, and met the enemy right in front. They were not twenty paces from us. We gave them a volley. Two companies of the German Legion were sent to keep them in play, whilst the lines were forming. Two brigades came up, at double quick time. We formed in three lines, and forced them to retire. They lost, in their fight, a great number of men by the fire of our cannon.

After dark, we withdrew our lines, and encamped in a wood. We were in great want of necessaries, having very little bread or beef amongst us, and no water. I set off in quest of some, slung round with canteens belonging to the mess. After searching about for a long time, faint and weary, I was going to give up in despair, and sat down to reflect what I should do. Numbers were moving around, looking anxiously for water of any kind, quality was of no moment. I thought I heard a bustle on my right. I leaped up, ran towards it; I heard voices and the croaking of frogs. Tempting sound! I stopped not to reflect. As I drew near, the sound became more distinct; I heard the welcome words, 'Water, water!' In I ran, up to the knees amongst mules and men, and, putting down my head, drank a sweet draught of it, dirty as it was, then filled my canteens, and came off quite happy. The croaking of the frogs was pleasanter music, at that time, and more welcome, than any other sound. When I came to the camp ground, I was welcomed with joy. We got our allowance of liquor, and mixed it with the water; then lay down, and slept till an hour before day, when we moved on to our old position on the hills. The French lay in column close by Salamanca. We remained there, till Lord Wellington perceived the French were endeavouring to get into our rear, to cut off our communications, they being very superior in force. The army received orders to draw up in column, and move on in brigades each brigade in succession, leaving the 71st for the rear guard.

I, at this time, got a post, being for fatigue, with other four. We were sent to break biscuit, and make a mess for Lord Wellington's hounds. I was very hungry, and thought it a good job at the time, as we got our own fill, while we broke the biscuit – a thing I had not got for some days. When thus engaged, the prodigal son never once was out of my mind; and I sighed as I fed the dogs, over my humble situation and ruined hopes.

As we followed the army, Colonel Cadogan made us halt in a plain upon ploughed land, where he began to drill us. We were wet and weary, and like to faint with hunger. The ground was so soft with the rain, we could scarce keep the step. The French were coming down from the heights. 'Now,' says he, ' there they are; if you are not quicker in your movements, I will leave you every one to them.' At this moment, General Hill's aid-de-camp rode up, saying, 'Move on, and cover the brigade of artillery, by the General's order, or you will be all prisoners in five minutes.' We immediately left off drill, and marched on, until dark, under a heavy rain, and over miserable roads; one shoe in our hand, the other on our knapsack.

As we entered a wood, we were agreeably annoyed by the grunting of hogs and squeaking of pigs. 'There is a town here,' says my comrade. We all longed for 'Pile arms.' At length the word was given, and cooks ordered to cut wood. More cooks than one turned out of each mess, and went in different directions in search of forage. All this time the whole wood resounded with the reports of muskets. It resembled a wood contested by the enemy. At length our cooks returned, one with a pig, another with a skin of wine, or with flour; and we made a hearty supper, and lay down happy and contented.

Next morning we continued the line of march, under a heavy rain; the horses were scarce able to drag the cannon through the mud. We marched thus, about eight miles, and halted at a village, where we encamped, and cooked the remains of our pork. Every one was engaged cooking or cutting wood, when the French made their appearance on the opposite heights. The bugle sounded to fall in; immediately we formed square, to receive cavalry. They galloped down close to our square. We had not time to load our pieces; and many of us were only half accoutred, they had come so quick upon us. Many of them were very much in liquor: three or four galloped into the centre of our square; we opened to receive them. A brigade of guns coming to our relief, they put to the right about, and fled. We stood under arms for some time. A brigade of French infantry was drawn up on the opposite heights. It being only their advanced guard, Lord Wellington gave orders to pile arms, but to remain accoutred. We stood in this position, the rain pouring upon us, until we were forced to lie down, through fatigue.

Day at length appearing, we got orders to move on, after the army, in sections; the enemy having retired through the night. We had not moved thus two miles, until the French advance came down upon us, picking up every individual who fell out. The cries of the women and children were dreadful, as we left them. We were retiring in square, playing a howitzer from the centre, to keep their cavalry in check. We continued to move on, in this manner, sending out the left company to fire and retire. The rain poured; the roads were knee-deep; when one had to stop, all were obliged to stop. Each of the enemy's cavalry had a foot-soldier behind him, who formed when they came close. When we were halted, and advanced to charge, they mounted and retired.

At length we forded the Aguida, and encamped on the opposite side. Rear-guards and quarter-guards were immediately sent out, and picquets planted. We were not an hour and a half encamped, when a dreadful firing commenced on our left. We were all under arms in a moment. The firing continued very severe, for the space of two hours. We then piled arms and began to cut wood, to lay under us, that the water might run below, as the rain continued to pour in torrents. We might as well have lain in the river. We were up an hour before day, and wrung out our blankets, emptied our shoes of the water, each man trembling like the leaf of a tree. We followed the line of march for about four leagues, and encamped in a plain, expecting to be attacked every moment. The French did not advance this night.

Next morning we were marched into a town. Sergeants were called out for quarters; and we were put in by sections, into the best quarters they could find. This town we called the *reeky* town; it was the most smoky place I ever was in. The sergeants got two months' pay for each man; every one had a little. Canteens were immediately in requisition; wine and *accadent* were the only words you could hear. Three dollar's for wine, and one for *accadent*, made a joyful night, and a merry mess. We had no care; the song went round: we were as merry as if we had not suffered in our retreat. The recollection of our wants made our present enjoyments doubly dear. Next morning we did the best we could to clean ourselves; but we made a very shabby figure. Our haversacks were black with grease; we could not get the marks of the pork out all we could do.

Here we remained eight days; then marched to Porto Banyes, where we received a draft of 150 men from England, and staid about eight days; then marched to Monte Moso. We got here a new kitt. Before this, we were completely in rags; and it used to be our daily labour to pick the vermin off ourselves. We were quartered in the villages, until Colonel Cadogan arrived from England, who inspected and reviewed us in our new clothes. We looked very well. The Colonel told us we were *as fat as fowls*.

During the time the 50th were in Boho, the French made an attempt to surprise it. We were marched up to it, at double-quick time. We ran up hill for four miles, and were formed in the town, and marched up to the walls, making as great a show as possible. The French stood in column, on the opposite side of the town. We had picquets of the 50th posted on the outside. Boho being a town of great trade, the French hoped to get a supply of clothing; but finding they could not succeed, they retired, and we went back to our old cantonments.

Goes into winter quarters at Boho – Manners of the Spanish peasants – Adventure in a churchyard – Description of the Fandango – Departure from Boho.

In a few days we relieved the 50th, and marched into Boho; in which place we remained all winter, till until the month of May 1813, when the campaign commenced.

I got a most excellent billet; every thing was in plenty; fruit in abundance. I was regarded as a son of the family;

partook with them at meals; and if any thing was better than another, my part was in it. I amused myself, when off duty, in teaching the children to read; for which my hosts thought they never could be grateful enough.

I have often thought the Spaniards resembled the Scots, in their manner of treating their children. How has my heart warmed, when I have seen the father, with his wife by his side, and the children round them, repeating the Lord's prayer and the 23rd Psalm at evening before they went to bed! Once a week, the children were catechised. When I told them they did the same in Scotland, they looked at me with astonishment, and asked, 'If heretics did so?' The priests often drew comparisons much to our disadvantage from the conduct of our men. They even said, every heretic in England was as bad as them.

One afternoon, I had walked into the churchyard; and, after having wandered through it, I lay down in the shade of the wall, near a grave that appeared to have been lately made. While lying thus, I heard a sob: I looked towards the place whence it came, and perceived a beautiful female kneeling beside a grave, devoutly counting her rosary, her tears falling fast upon the ground. I lay, afraid to move, lest the noise might disturb her. She remained for some time, absorbed in devotion, then rose from her knees, and taking a small jar of holy water, sprinkled the grave, and retired undisturbed by me. I mentioned the circumstance to no one; but, day after day, I was an unperceived witness of this scene. At length she saw me as she approached, and was retiring in haste. I came near her. She stood to let me pass. I said, 'My presence shall give you no uneasiness: Adieu.' 'Stay,' she said, 'are you Don Galves' good soldier?'

I replied, 'I live with him.' 'Stay, you can feel for me; I have none to feel for, nor advise me. Blessed Virgin, be my friend!' She looked to heaven, her eyes beaming resignation and hope, the tears dropping on her bosom. I stretched out my hand to her; my eyes, I believe, were wet, I did not speak. 'None,' she said, mournfully, 'can again have any hand: I gave it to Francisco.' ''Tis the hand of friendship.' 'I can have no friend but death – You do not pray for the dead; you cannot pray with me.' I said, 'I will listen to yours.' She then began her usual prayers; then rose, and sprinkled the grave with holy water. I inquired, 'Whose grave do you water?' 'My mother's.' 'How long has she been dead?' 'Five years.' 'Five years! have you done thus so long?' 'Alas, no! my mother had been released; but, five weeks ago, my mournful task again began; 'tis for Francisco. Adieu,' she sobbed, and retired with a hurried step. I dare not embellish lest this incident should not be credited; but I feel this a cold account of what passed. I have not taken away, neither have I added a word that did not pass between us. From Galves, I learnt that Francisco had fallen in a Guerilla party. It is the belief in Spain, that every drop of holy water sprinkled upon the grave, quenches a flame in purgatory.

We had passed the winter in an agreeable manner. We lived well: the inhabitants were on good terms with us: we had every thing in abundance; and amusements were not wanting. We had bull-fights, at which we used to exhibit our powers. Several of our men were hurt. Our horsemen were particularly good bull-fighters; and the women used to give them great praise. Often we had dancings in the evening; sometimes we got two or three of our band, and then we had dancing in style. Wine and mirth we never wanted: music was our great want.

The peasants used to dance to the sound of their rattles, consisting of two pieces of hard wood, which they meld between their fingers, and by shaking their hands, kept time, in the same manner as the boys in Edinburgh and other parts, play what they call 'cockledum ditt.' – They call them castanetts.

They have one dance which I never saw in any other place: they call it fandango. I can hardly say it is a dance, for it is scarcely decent. The dancers first run to each other, as if they are looking for one another; then the woman runs away, the man follows; next he runs, and she follows. This they do alternately, all the time using the most expressive gestures, until both seem overcome; when they retire, and another couple take their place. This dance had a great effect upon us; but the Spaniards saw it without being moved, and laughed at the quick breathing and amorous looks of our men.

The winter in Boho was the shortest I ever passed in Spain; yet we remained in that town until May 1813. The only disagreeable thing was, that the wolves, which were very numerous, used to visit us at our advanced posts, when on duty through the night.

One night, while on duty at the bridge, I thought I was to have fallen a prey to a very large wolf. My orders were to be on the alert, and if I heard the least sound, to place my ear upon the ground, to distinguish if it were the tread of men or of horses, and give the alarm. The night was starry, and a little cloudy, when, about half past one o'clock, I could distinguish the tread of an animal. I believed it to be a stray mule, or ass; but at length could distinguish a large wolf, a few yards from the bridge, in the middle of the road, looking full upon me. I levelled my piece, and stood; my eyes fixed on his: I durst not fire, lest I should miss him, and give a false alarm. I expected him every moment to spring upon me. We stood thus looking upon each other, until the tread of the sergeant and guard to relieve me were heard; then the beast scampered off; and relieved me from my disagreeable situation.

May came at length, and we were obliged to leave our kind hosts. I never before felt regret at quitting a town in Spain. That morning we marched, the town was deserted by its inhabitants, who accompanied us a good way; girls weeping, and running into the ranks to be protected from their parents, and hanging upon their old acquaintances; parents tearing away and scolding their children; soldiers and inhabitants singing, or exchanging adieus. Almost every man had his handkerchief on the muzzle of his firelock. Don Galves' children, weeping, took leave of me. I never saw them again. May God bless them.

4

BATTLE of Vittoria – Arrival before Pamplona – Skirmish in front of Maya – Battles in the Pyrenees – Battle before Pamplona – Sufferings of our army on the heights – Crosses the Nive – Battle of Bayonne – Severe fighting before Aris.

At length we were left to reflect upon our absent friends, and commence the toils of war afresh. We lay in camp until the whole army joined; then were reviewed by Lord Wellington, and received orders to take the line of march, and follow the enemy.

We marched over a great part of Spain, quite across the country; many parts of which were very beautiful, more particularly that before we crossed the Ebro. But we were so harassed by fatigue in our long marches, that we never left the camp, and were too weary to pay much attention to any thing that did not relieve our wants.

We continued to advance, until the 20th of June; when, reaching the neighbourhood of Vittoria, we encamped upon the face of a hill. Provisions were very scarce. We had not a bit of tobacco, and were smoking leaves and herbs. Colonel Cadogan rode away, and got us half a pound of tobacco a man, which was most welcome.

Next morning we got up as usual. The first pipes played for parade; the second did not play at the usual time. We began to suspect all was not right. We remained thus until eleven o'clock then received orders to fall in, and follow the line of march. During our march we fell to one side, to allow a brigade of guns to pass us at full speed 'Now' said my comrades, 'we will have work to do before night.' We crossed a river; and, as we passed through a village, we saw on the other side of the road, the French camp, and their fires still burning. just as they had left them. Not a shot had been fired at this time. We observed a large Spanish column moving along the heights, on our right. We halted, and drew up in column. Orders were given to brush out our locks, oil them, and examine our flints. We being in the rear, these were soon followed by orders to open out from the centre, to allow the 71st to advance. Forward we moved up the hill. The firing was now very heavy. Our rear had not engaged, before word came for the Doctor to assist Colonel Cadogan, who was wounded. Immediately we marched up the hill, the piper playing, 'Hey Johnny Cope.' The French had possession of the top, but we soon forced them back, and drew up in column on the height; Sending out four companies to our left to skirmish. The remainder moved on to the opposite height. As we advanced driving them before us, a French officer, a pretty fellow, was pricking and forcing his men to stand. They heeded him not – he was very harsh: – 'Down with him' cried one near me ; and down he fell pierced by more than one ball.

Scarce were we upon the height, when a heavy column, dressed in great-coats, with white covers on their hats, exactly resembling the Spanish, gave us a volley, which put us to the right-about at double-quick time down the hill, the French close behind, through the whins. The four companies got the word, the French were on them. They likewise thought them Spaniards, until they got a volley that killed or wounded almost every man of them. We retired to the height, covered by the 50th, who gave the pursuing column a volley which checked their speed. We moved up the remains of our shattered regiment to the height. Being in great want of ammunition, we were again served with sixty rounds a man, and kept up our fire for some time, until the bugle sounded to cease firing.

We lay on the height for some time. Our drought was excessive; there was no water upon the height, save one small spring, which was rendered useless. One of our men, in the heat of the action, called out he would have a drink, let the world go as it would. He stooped to drink; a ball pierced his head; he fell with it in the well, which was discoloured by brains and blood – thirsty as we were, we could not taste it.

At this time the Major had the command, our second Colonel [Charles Cother[1]] being wounded. There were not 300 of us on the height able to do duty, out of above 1000 who drew rations in the morning.[2] The cries of the wounded were most heart-rending.

The French, on the opposite height, were getting under arms: we could give no assistance, as the enemy appeared to be six to one of us. Our orders were to maintain the height while there was a man of us. The word was given to shoulder arms. The French, at the same moment, got under arms. The engagement began in the plains. The French were amazed, and soon put to the right-about, through Vittoria. We followed, as quick as our weary limbs would carry us. Our legs were full of thorns, and our feet bruised upon the roots of the trees. Coming to a bean field at the bottom of the heights, immediately the column was broke, and every man filled his haversack. We continued to advance until it was dark, and then encamped on a height above Vittoria.

This was the dullest encampment I ever made. We had left 700 men behind.[3] None spoke; each hung his head, mourning the loss of a friend and comrade. About twelve o'clock, a man of each company was sent to receive half a pound of flour for each man, at the rate of our morning's strength; so that there was more than could be used by those who had escaped. I had fired 108 rounds this day. Next morning we awoke, dull, stiff, and weary. I could scarce touch my head with my right hand; my shoulder was as black as coal. We washed out our firelocks, and moved off again about twelve o'clock, in the line of march.

Towards the afternoon of the 22nd, the day after the battle of Vittoria, a great number of our men joined, who had made their escape, after being taken the day before.[4] We encamped, and passed a night of congratulation; mutual hardships made us all brothers. The slain were forgot, in our joy for those we had gained thus unexpectedly. Next morning, we made a more respectable appearance on parade, being now about 800 strong. The day following, we continued our march. In the afternoon, we had a dreadful storm of thunder and rain. A Portuguese officer and his horse were killed by it. We encamped upon the face of a hill, the rain continuing to pour. The storm not abating, we could not get our tents up, and were exposed all night to its violence.

Next day, we arrived before Pamplona, where we lay for some time. One night we were ordered under arms at twelve o'clock. The report was, that Pamplona was to be stormed. We marched until day-break, then drew up in a hollow in the rear of the town, when we got orders to fall back to our camp ground.

Soon after, we were relieved by a division of Spanish, and marched towards the Pyrenees, where we soon fell in with our old playfellows the French, and had a very severe skirmish in the front of the village of Maya. The regiment was divided into two columns; the right commanded by Major Walker,[5] the left by Major M'Kenzie.[6] We remained under arms all night, the French keeping up their fire. Next morning we forced them over the heights, into their own country in style; then encamped.

Fatigue parties were called to make rows and rain-works. Our two rear companies were appointed to move to the heights in the rear, upon the first alarm, and maintain them while a man should remain. The signal was three great guns; on the report of the first of which, every man was to stand to his arms. One day we sent out a fatigue party, to cut wood to make arms-racks. They were not come back when a gun was fired. We stood to our arms, making ready to engage. It was a false alarm.

Our fatigue parties were out for forage, and we were busy cooking, when the signal was given on the 25th July. The two rear companies moved to the heights, the rest of the regiment to the alarm-post, where we had work enough upon our arrival. The French were in great force, moving up the heights in solid column. We killed great numbers of them in their advance; but they still moved on. We were forced to give way, and continued thus to retire, maintaining every height to the last, contesting every foot of ground. At length we were forced to the height where our old quarter-guard used to be posted. We maintained our position against them a considerable time; during which, we had the mortification to see the French making merry in our camp, eating the dinner we had cooked for ourselves. What could we do? – they were so much superior in numbers.

I have often admired the bravery of the French officers. This day, while I was in the rear guard, covering the retreat, about two dozen of us were pursued and molested by a company of the French. Out of breath, and unable to run farther, we cried, 'Let us make a stand and get breath, else we will never reach the top.' 'Take your will,' returned the officers. Immediately we faced about the French halted; their officers pricked them on. We formed front, across the road, and charged the French officers in the rear urging their troops forward. All would not do; the men forced their officers fairly over the hill, and ran. We had what we wished, an unmolested retreat, and moved slowly up the height. We were then joined by a brigade of Brunswickers, – gave three cheers, and charged the French along the heights, keeping up our fire till dark. A part of the regiment made fires, while the remainder kept their ground upon the main height, until about twelve o'clock. We then marched off towards the Black Forest, leaving our wounded, whose cries were piercing; but we could not help them. Numbers continued to follow us, crawling on their hands and knees, filling the air with their groans. Many, who could not do so, held out their hands, supplicating to be taken with us. We tore ourselves away, and hurried to get out of sight. We could not bear it.

The roads were very bad, the rain continued to pour, and we made but little way. At day-break, we formed on the outside of Maya, and got orders to cook; but scarce had we begun when the French made their appearance. We immediately moved on to a stronger height on the opposite side, and encamped. Here we got three days allowance of beef and bread served out to each man, and an allowance of liquor. As soon as cooking was over, we marched on to the Black Forest, and never halted, until two o'clock in the morning. The night was dark and stormy. The wounded officers were carried in blankets on the shoulders of the men. The wounded soldiers who had been enabled still to keep up with us, made the heart bleed at their cries; while the forcing up of the baggage caused such a noise, that the whole was a scene of misery and confusion. We halted to allow the baggage to get forward.

Shortly after day-light, the French advance came up with our rear-guard, consisting of a brigade of Portuguese, which continued to skirmish all the way through the forest. We lost a great number of men in this forest, unable to keep up through illness and fatigue, and not a few from the effects of liquor. It was found necessary to stave the stores of liquor; and the men were carrying it away in their bonnets. Many were intoxicated, and carried upon the shoulders of their comrades.

We at length got out of the forest and encamped. Picquets were posted, and we began to cook; but we had scarcely commenced, when the French were again upon us. The camp was moved, and we marched until two hours after dark. We were then drawn up in column, and lay down on the bare ground, until next morning. The French moved about two miles, and then turned off on their left, towards Pamplona, thinking there was nothing to stop them. We remained here until morning.

Day was scarce broke, when we heard three guns fire towards our right. All were under arms in a moment; and we stood, in this situation, a considerable time. The noise of artillery and musketry was incessant on our right; but, towards the afternoon, the firing ceased, and the French were forced from the heights opposite Pamplona. After Lord Wellington had defeated them, they retreated by our right.

We got orders to occupy a height in the wood. Two companies were sent, at extended order, down the wood, where we were not long before the enemy began to appear; and the firing commenced with their skirmishers. After doing our utmost for some time, we were forced to retire to the top of the height; and, when we arrived upon it, they were so numerous, it was vain to contend. We gave them two or three volleys, and retired through a small village, they following close in the rear: then we drew up, along the side of a strong rock, close by the main road, determined to defend it to the last. Lord Wellington sent a division to our assistance. The enemy seeing them approach, drew up, and continued to annoy us for some time; then fell back upon the village, and encamped. There were some fine fields of grain here, which they set fire to. We lay down, fatigued and weary, having been constantly engaged almost the whole afternoon.

Chapter 4

Next morning, the 5th of August, the enemy began to retire, we following close at their heels through the Black Forest. They retired back into France. We halted upon our old camp-ground for the space of half an hour, and then returned to our old quarters at Maya. We were very melancholy, the whole bringing to our minds the time when we last left it and our wounded and dying comrades.

After encamping on a height on the other side, for two or three days, we were marched round to the heights of Roncesvalles, where we encamped, relieving a brigade of the 7th division. We lay here for a considerable time, working like galley slaves from morning till evening, in building batteries and block-houses. All the time I had been a soldier, my labour could not stand in the least comparison with, my fatigues at this time.

Orders were given that the heights should be kept by the 3rd and 4th division, week about. We retired, moving down, and encamped on the other side of the village.

A short time afterwards, we got orders for duty on the heights on the opposite side, of which we were glad, thinking that the work would not be so severe. But we were disagreeably undeceived. Our labour was incessant; every day, we were either on guard or on fatigue. All the time we remained here, we were not a night in bed out of two; besides, the weather was dreadful; we had always either snow or hail, the hail often as large as nuts. We were forced to keep our knapsacks on our heads, to protect us from its violence. The mules, at these times, used to run crying up and down, hurt by the stones. The frost was most severe, accompanied by high winds. Often, for whole days and nights, we could not get a tent to stand. Many of us were frost-bitten, and others were found dead at their posts. At this time, I cursed my hard fate, and groaned over my folly. Frequently have I been awakened, through the night, by the sobs of those around me in the tent; more especially by the young soldiers, who had not been long from their mothers fire-sides. They often spent the darkness of the night in tears. The weather was so dreadful, the 92nd regiment got grey trowsers served out to them: they could not live with their kilts; the cold would have killed them.

In about two days after we went down to the valley, the day being good, the French came down from the heights nearest France. General Stewart[7] being there, at the same time, with our advanced post, and seeing their manoeuvres, ordered us to advance towards them. We soon beat them back, and retired to our post. A few days afterwards, the weather was so very bad, that great numbers of the men fell sick. We were then forced to leave the heights, and encamp in the valley; leaving strong picquets in the block houses on the main pass, which were relieved daily. Fatigue parties were sent up to work, nevertheless, every day the weather would permit. At this time we buried two guns of Captain Mitchell's brigade of artillery, which displeased him much. Through intercession, General Stewart ordered up a fatigue-party to raise them again. We were covered by the picquets, and, with great difficulty, at length got them raised and brought down to the valley. Each man on fatigue got an extra allowance of grog, the only welcome recompense.

We lay here for some time, frequently attacked in the block-houses by the French, and at length received orders to leave our purgatory in the heights, and move round towards Maya. We marched that whole afternoon, and all night, until next morning; when the whole army formed on the other side of Maya. We were appointed the brigade of reserve, being far in the rear, and very much fatigued. An attack was begun, almost as soon as we arrived. We moved towards the enemy's works, which were very strong; but we forced them out, then moved round to our own right, the remainder of the army pursuing them. Their camp-ground, which was hutted like a little town, was occupied by us during the night.

November 10. – We, next morning, continued to move to our own right, until we came to a village called Cambo; on the outside of which the enemy had batteries planted, and strong works. We kept up a severe fire, for some time, but could not storm their works, on account of the depth of the intrenchments. They found out that the Spanish troops under Morillo were fording the river on their right. We retired back into camp, and lay there two days: the weather was so bad we could not move out.

In the afternoon, they blew up the bridge over the Nive, and retired out of the town. We then marched into it; and were cantoned, and lay there for a considerable time; the French on one side, and we on the other; our sentinel and theirs on the bridge, not five yards asunder. The night before we crossed, the French came down to the banks of the river with their music, and gave us a tune or two. We thought to change their tune before next night. We were then to be all under arms at a minute's notice.

About nine o'clock, the whole of our in-lying picquets were called to cover a party of sappers and miners, in raising a battery to cover our fording ground; and the sentinel on the broken bridge received orders to shoot the French sentinel, on the first gun for alarm being fired. Both were walking from one parapet to another; the Frenchman unconscious of any unusual danger; the English sentinel listening, and often looking to the victim, his heart revolting from the deed he dared not disobey. The match touched the signal gun; next moment the French sentinel fell into the river, pierced by a ball.

As soon as the sappers and miners had constructed the battery, we moved back into the town, and remained until an hour before day. We were drawn up on our fording ground; orders were given that not a man should speak above his breath. The whole being prepared, the word was given to pass the river, when three guns were fired on our left. Our right wing was sent out to cover the fording. The left forded the river; but we had not reached the opposite bank, when we received a volley from the enemy's picquets. We gave three cheers, – splashed through the water; they retired, and we pursued them. The regiment formed upon the top of the height, sending out two companies to follow the enemy close; but they never came up with them.

All the night of the 11th of December, we lay in camp upon the face of a height, near the Spaniards. In the afternoon of the 12th, we received orders to move round towards Bayonne, where we were quartered along the main road. There we remained a few days, until we received orders to march to our own right, to assist a Spanish force, who were engaged with superior numbers. We set off by day-light, in the morning of the 13th, towards them, and were moving on, when General Hill sent an aide-de-camp after us, saying, 'That is not the direction, – follow me.' We put to the right about, to the main road towards Bayonne. We soon came to the scene of action, and were immediately engaged. We had continued firing, without intermission, for five hours, advancing and retreating, and lost a great number of men, but could not gain a bit of ground. Towards evening, we were relieved by a brigade which belonged to another division. As many of us as could be collected were drawn up. General Hill gave us great praise for our behaviour this day, and ordered an extra allowance of liquor to each man. We were marched back to our old quarters along the road-side.

The day's service had been very severe, but now I took it with the coolest indifference I felt no alarm; it was all of course. I began to think my body charmed. My mind had come to that pass, I took every thing as it came, without a thought. If I was at ease, with plenty, I was happy; if in the midst of the enemy's fire, or of the greatest privations, I was not concerned. I had been in so many changes of plenty and want, ease and danger, they had ceased to be anticipated either with joy or fear.

We lay upon the road-side for two or three days, having two companies three leagues to the rear, carrying the wounded to the hospital. We were next cantoned three leagues above Bayonne, along the side of the river. We had strong picquets planted along the banks. The French were cantoned upon the other side. Never a night passed that we were not molested by boats passing up and down the river, with provisions and necessaries to the town. Our orders were, to turn out, and keep up a constant fire upon them while passing. We had two grasshopper guns planted upon the side of the river; by means of which we one night sunk a boat loaded with clothing for the army, setting it on fire with, red-hot shot.

Next day we were encamped in the rear of the town, being relieved by a brigade of Portuguese. We remained in camp two or three days, expecting to be attacked, the enemy having crossed above us on the river. We posted picquets in the town, near our camp. At length, receiving orders to march, we moved on, until we came to a river on our right, which ran very swift. Part of the regiment having crossed, we got orders to come to the right-about, and we marched back to our old camp-ground. Next morning, we received orders to take another road towards Salvatero; where we encamped that night, and remained until the whole army assembled the following day.

About two o'clock, in the afternoon, we were under arms, and moved towards the river, covered by a brigade of artillery. We forded and continued to skirmish, alongst the heights, until the town was taken. We lost only one man during the whole time. We encamped upon the other side of the town; and next morning followed the line of march, until we came before a town called Aris. We had severe fighting before we got into it. We were led on by an aid-de-camp. The contest lasted until after dark. We planted picquets in different streets of the town; the enemy did the same in others. Different patroles were sent out during the night; but the French were always found on the alert. They retired before day-light; and we marched into the town, with our music at the head of the regiments. The town appeared then quite desolate not worth two-pence; but we were not three days in it, until the French inhabitants came back, opened their shops and houses, and it became a fine lively place. There was a good deal of plundering the first night; for the soldiers, going into the houses, and finding no person within, helped themselves. The people have a way of keeping their fowls in cans full of grease, about the size of a hen. This we found out by accident; for, wanting some grease to fry, in cooking, we took one of these cans and cut out the fowl. We commenced a search for the grease cans, and were very successful. The fowls were excellent. We lay there a considerable time, then were marched towards Toulouse, and halted at a village four leagues from it, with orders to turn out on a moments notice. We were drawn out at twelve o'clock at night, and marched close up to the town, designing to throw a bridge over the river; but it ran so swift, that we failed in our attempt. We then kindled fires in all quarters, and returned to the village. Next morning, we marched round towards the main road to Toulouse, and were cantoned along the road. We lay here for some time, and were, every morning under arms an hour before day.

— ♦ —

BATTLE of Toulouse – Remarkable occurrence – Returns to Ireland – Embarked for North America – Returns to England – Sails for Antwerp – Marched to Leuse – Arrival at Waterloo.

At length, on the 10th of April, we received orders to attack Toulouse, and moved on by another road, on the opposite side from the one we had lain upon. We were drawn up in column, in rear of a house, and remained there for some time, sending out the flank companies to skirmish; and, at length, forced the enemy back upon their works. The contest now began to be more severe. A brigade of guns coming up, played upon their works for some time, and then retired, night coming on. We were posted in the different streets of the suburbs, to watch the enemy's motions. At last we got our allowance of liquor served out, and retired to our cantonement.

I shall ever remember an adventure that happened to me, towards the afternoon. We were in extended order, firing and retiring. I had just risen to run behind my file, when a spent shot struck me on the groin, and took the breath from me. 'God receive my soul!' I said, and sat down resigned. The French were advancing fast. I laid my musket down, and gasped for breath. I was sick and put my canteen to my head, but could not taste the water: however, I washed my mouth, and grew less faint. I looked to my thigh, and seeing no blood, took resolution to put my hand to the part to feel the wound. My hand was unstained by blood; but the part was so painful that I could not touch it. At this moment of helplessness the French came up. One of them made a charge at me, as I sat pale as death. In another moment I would have been transfixed, had not his next man forced the point past me: 'Do not touch the good Scot,' said he; and then addressing himself to me, added, 'Do you remember me?' I had not recovered my breath sufficiently to speak distinctly: I answered, 'No.' – 'I saw you at Sobral,' he replied. Immediately I recognised him to be a soldier whose life I had saved from a Portuguese, who was going to kill him as he lay wounded. 'Yes, I know you,' I replied. – 'God bless you!'

cried he; and, giving me a pancake out of his hat, moved on with his fellows; the rear of whom took my knapsack, and left me lying. I had fallen down for greater security. I soon recovered so far as to walk, though with pain, and joined the regiment next advance.

We were quartered in wine stores; where we lay for a considerable time, sending out a regiment, each night, on duty. The 71st happened to be the regiment on duty, on the night in which the French evacuated Toulouse. We immediately gave notice, and marched into the town; halted half an hour, until the cavalry passed through it, and then moved on after them. We fell in with a number of the enemy's sick and wounded, whom we sent back to the town. We halted at Villa Franca, and were cantoned. Soult lay in a town on the heights in front, about one league and a half from us.

We remained here two or three days; when we were all turned out, cavalry and artillery, the French being under arms. Three guns were fired. The French did not seem inclined to attack us. We were encamped again. In the course of the day, flags of truce were passing between the armies. At length, General Soult came in his carriage, guarded by a squadron of his cavalry. We then got word that Buonaparte was deposed, and we were soon to have peace. – Joy beamed on every face, and made every tongue eloquent. We sang and drank that whole night, and talked of home. Next morning, falling back to Toulouse, we were cantoned there, and lay for a long time, looking anxiously for orders to embark for England. At length we marched to Bordeaux, were reviewed by Lord Wellington, and embarked for Ireland.

We arrived at Cork in June 1814. I had now been seven years and eleven months a soldier, and therefore hoped for my discharge. I had still one year to serve, although enlisted for seven. Being only sixteen years of age, my seven years were counted from my eighteenth. Had I called myself seventeen, I should have now been free; but I scorned to lie: neither was I aware of this circumstance.

This episode is fictional; because his discharge was imminent, Joseph Sinclair was transferred to the home service second battalion of the regiment, which was about to be disbanded. James Todd on the other hand still had some time to run on his enlistment and so, unlike Sinclair, went to Waterloo.[8]

Upon our arrival at Cork, we were marched to Limerick, and lay there a long time; then got the route for Cork to embark for America. I wanted but a few months to be free. I sought my discharge, but was refused. I was almost tempted to desert. I lamented my becoming a soldier, at this time, more than I had done on the retreat, or upon the Pyrenees. To be so near home, and almost free, and yet to be sent across the Atlantic, was very galling. I knew not what to do. I kept my honour, and embarked. What vexed me, was some being discharged who had not been so long soldiers as I had been; only they were above eighteen when they enlisted.

We lay on board six weeks before setting sail. When on our way, a schooner fired a gun and brought us to, and gave us orders for Deal. My heart bounded with joy: Freedom, freedom!' – I would not have taken a thousand pounds to stay, – I would have left the army without a shirt. I was oppressed all the time I was on board; my mind dwelt on nothing but home. If any one asked a question or spoke to me, I was so absent that I seldom answered to the point. After the ship was put about for England, a load was taken from my mind, and I became more happy. We landed all our heavy baggage at Deal, then sailed round to Gravesend, and disembarked. We lay there only one afternoon, then were put on board the smacks, and were landed at Antwerp.

Next morning we were marched to Louis, [*Leuse*], where we lay, quartered in the different villages around, until the 16th of June 1815. We used to be drilled every day. We were going out, for a field-day, on the 16th, when we were ordered back and formed on one side of the village, We stopped here a short time; then were sent to quarters to pack up every thing and march. We immediately marched off towards the French frontier. We had a very severe march of sixteen miles, excepting to halt and be quartered in every town through which we passed. We knew not where we were marching. About one o'clock in the morning, we were halted in a village. A brigade of Brunswickers marching out, we took their quarters, hungry and weary.

Next morning, the 17th, we got our allowance of liquor, and moved on until the heat of the day; when we encamped, and our baggage was ordered to take the high road to Brussels. We sent out fatigue parties for water, and set a cooking. Our fires were not well kindled, when we got orders to fall in, and move on along the high road towards Waterloo. The whole length of the road was very much crowded by artillery and ammunition-carts, all advancing towards Waterloo. The troops were much embarrassed in marching, the roads were so crowded. As soon as we arrived on the ground, we formed in column. The rain began to pour. The firing had never ceased all yesterday and today, at a distance. We encamped and began to cook; when the enemy came in sight, and again spoiled our cooking. We advanced towards them. When we reached the height they retired, which caused the whole army to get under arms and move to their positions. Night coming on, we stood under arms for some time. The army then retired to their own rear, and lay down under arms, leaving the 71st in advance. During the whole night, the rain never ceased. Two hours after day-break, General Hill came down, taking away the left subdivision of the 10th company to cover his reconnaissance. Shortly afterwards, we got half an allowance of liquor, which was the most welcome thing I ever received. I was so stiff and sore from the rain, I could not move with freedom for some time. A little afterwards, the weather clearing up, we began to clean our arms, and prepare for action. The whole of the opposite heights were covered by the enemy.

— ◆ —

BATTLE of Waterloo – March to Paris – Anecdotes there – Gets his discharge, and returns to Scotland – Conclusion.

A young lad, who had joined but a short time before, said to me, while we were cleaning: 'Tom, you are an old soldier, and have escaped often, and have every chance to escape this time also. I am sure I am to fall' – 'Nonsense, be not gloomy' – 'I am certain,' he said: 'All I ask is, that you will tell my parents, when you get home, that I ask God's pardon for the evil I have done, and the grief I have given them. Be sure to tell I died praying for their blessing and pardon.' I grew dull myself, but gave him all the heart I could. He only shook his head: I could say nothing to alter his belief.

The artillery had been tearing away, since daybreak, in different parts of the line. About twelve o'clock we received orders to fall in for attack. We then marched up to our position, where we lay on the face of a brae, covering a brigade of guns. – We were so overcome by the fatigue of the two day's march, that, scarce had we lain down until many of us fell asleep. I slept sound for some time, while the cannon-balls, plunging in amongst us, killed a great many. I was suddenly awakened. A ball struck the ground a little below me, turned me heels-over-head, broke my musket in pieces, and killed a lad at my side. I was stunned and confused, and knew not whether I was wounded or not. I felt a numbness in my arm for some time.

We lay thus, about an hour and a half, under a dreadful fire, which cost us about 60 men, while we had never fired a shot. The balls were falling thick amongst us. The young man I lately spoke of lost his legs by a shot at this time. They were cut very close: he soon bled to death. 'Tom,' said he, 'remember your charge: my mother wept sore when my brother died in her arms. Do not tell her all how I died; if she saw me thus, it would break her heart: farewell, God bless my parents!' He said no more, his lips quivered, and he ceased to breathe.

About two o'clock, a squadron of lancers came down, hurraing, to charge the brigade of guns: they knew not what was in the rear. General Barnes[9] gave the word, 'Form square.' In a moment the whole brigade were on their feet, ready to receive the enemy. The General said, 'Seventy-first, I have often heard of your bravery, I hope it will not be worse than it has been, to-day.' Down they came upon our square. We soon put them to the right-about.

Shortly after we received orders to move to the heights. Onwards we marched, and stood, for a short time, in square; receiving cavalry every now and then. The noise and smoke were dreadful. At this time I could see but a very little way from me; but, all around, the wounded and slain lay very thick. We then moved on in column, for a considerable way, and formed line; gave three cheers, fired a few volleys, charged the enemy, and drove them back.

At this moment a squadron of cavalry rode furiously down upon our line. Scarce had we time to form. The square was only complete in front when they were upon the points of our bayonets. Many of our men were out of place. There was a good deal of jostling, for a minute or two, and a good deal of laughing. Our quarter-master lost his bonnet, in riding into the square; got it up, put it on, back foremost, and wore it thus all day. Not a moment had we to regard our dress. A French General lay dead in the square; he had a number of ornaments upon his breast. Our men fell to plucking them off, pushing each other as they passed, and snatching at them.

We stood in square for some time, whilst the 13th dragoons and a squadron of French dragoons were engaged. The 13th dragoons retiring to the rear of our column, we gave the French a volley, which put them to the right-about; then the 13th at them again. They did this for some time; we cheering the 13th, and feeling every blow they received. When a Frenchman fell, we shouted; and when one of the 13th, we groaned. We wished to join them, but were forced to stand in square.

The whole army retired to the heights in the rear; the French closely pursuing to our formation, where we stood, four deep, for a considerable time. As we fell back, a shot cut the straps of the knapsack of one near me: it fell, and was rolling away. He snatched it up, saying, 'I am not to lose you that way, you are all I have in the world;' tied it on the best manner he could, and marched on.

Lord Wellington came riding up. We formed square, with him in our centre, to receive cavalry. Shortly the whole army received orders to advance. We moved forwards in two columns, four deep, the French retiring at the same time. We were charged several times in our advance. This was our last effort; nothing could impede us. The whole of the enemy retired, leaving their guns and ammunition, and every other thing behind. We moved on towards a village, and charged right through, killing great numbers, the village was so crowded. We then formed on the other side of it, and lay down under the canopy of heaven, hungry and wearied to death. We had been oppressed, all day, by the weight of our blankets and great coats, which were drenched with rain, and lay upon our shoulders like logs of wood.

Scarce was my body stretched upon the ground, when sleep closed my eyes. Next morning, when I awoke, I was quite stupid. The whole night my mind had been harassed by dreams. I was fighting and charging, re-acting the scenes of the day, which were strangely jumbled with the scenes I had been in before. I rose up and looked around, and began to recollect. The events of the 18th came before me, one by one; still they were confused, the whole appearing as an unpleasant dream. My comrades began to awake and talk of it; then the events were embodied as realities. Many an action had I been in, wherein the individual exertions of our regiment had been much greater, and our fighting more severe; but never had I been where the firing was so dreadful, and the noise so great. When I looked over the field of battle, it was covered and heaped in many places; figures moving up and down upon it. The wounded crawling along the rows of dead, was a horrible spectacle; yet I looked on with less concern, I must say, at the moment, than I have felt at an accident, when in quarters. I have been sad at the burial of a comrade who died of sickness in the hospital, and followed him almost in tears; yet have I seen, after a battle, fifty men put into the same trench, and comrades amongst them, almost with indifference. I looked over the field of Waterloo as a matter of course – a matter of small concern.

In the morning we got half an allowance of liquor; and remained here until mid-day, under arms; then received orders to cook. When cooking was over, we marched on towards France. Nothing particular happened before reaching Paris, where we lay in the lines until the French capitulated. We had our posts planted at each side of the city. The French troops retired; and we got under arms and marched towards the gates. We had a cannon on each side of the gate, and gunners, with lighted matches, standing by them. We marched into the city; passed Lord Wellington, who stood at the gates, and were encamped on the main road to the Tuilleries, where we remained all the time we were here.

In marching through the city, a lad, dressed as a Frenchman, was looking up the companies very anxiously. One of our men said, 'Knock the French fellow down.' 'Dinna be sae fast, man,' said he. We stared to hear broad Scotch in Paris at this time. 'I am looking for my cousin,' he added, naming him: but he had been left behind, wounded.

When we were in camp before the Tuilleries, the first day, two girls were looking very eagerly up and down the regiment, when we were on parade. 'Do you wish a careless husband, my dear?' said one of our lads. – 'May be; will you be't?' said a Glasgow voice. 'Where the devil do you come from?' said the rough fellow. 'We're Paisley lasses; this is our regiment: we want to see if there's ony body here we ken.' The soldier, who was a Glasgow lad, could not speak. There is a music in our native tongue, in a foreign land, where it is not to be looked for, that often melts the heart when we hear it unexpectedly. These two girls had found their way from Paisley to Paris, and were working at tambouring, and did very well.

We lay three months in Paris. All that time I saw very little of it: I did not care to ask leave from the camp. At length we were marched to Flanders, to winter-quarters; and I got my discharge. I left my comrades with regret, but the service with joy.

I came down to the coast to embark, with light steps and a joyful heart, singing, '*When wild war's deadly blast was blawn.*' I was poor as poor could be; but I had hope before me, and pleasing dreams of home. I had saved nothing this campaign; and the money I had before was all gone. Government found me the means of getting to Edinburgh.

Hope and joy were my companions until I entered the Firth. I was on deck; the morning began to dawn; the shores of Lothian began to rise out of the mist. 'There is the land of cakes,' said the captain. A sigh escaped me; recollections crowded upon me – painful recollections. I went below to conceal my feelings, and never came up until the vessel was in the harbour. I ran from her, and hid myself in a public-house. All the time I had been away was forgot. I felt as if I had been in Leith the day before. I was so foolish as to think I would be known, and laughed at. In about half an hour I reasoned myself out of my foolish notions: but I could not bring myself to go up the Walk to Edinburgh. I went by the Easter Road. Every thing was strange to me, so many alterations had taken place; yet I was afraid to look any person in the face, lest he should recognise me. I was suffering as keenly at this moment as when I went away: I felt my face burning with shame.

At length I reached the door of the last house I had been in, before leaving Edinburgh. I had no power to knock: happy was it for me that I did not. A young girl came into the stair. I asked her if Mrs— lived there? 'No,' she said, 'she had flitted long ago.' 'Where does she live?' 'I do not know.' Where to go, I knew not. I came down stairs, and recognised a sign which had been in the same place before I went away. In I went, and inquired. The landlord knew me. – 'Tom,' said he, 'are you come back safe? – Poor fellow! give me your hand.' 'Does my mother live?' – 'Yes, yes; come in, and I will send for her, not to let the surprise be too great.' Away he went. I could not remain, but followed him; and, the next minute, I was in the arms of my mother.

I have been with my mother these fourteen months. She is sinking fast to the grave. I am happy I am here to lay her head in it. – Jeanie has been married these five years; and goes between her own and her mother's house, to take care of her. – John is in London, following out his business – William has been in Glasgow.

LETTER BY THE WRITER OF THE JOURNAL TO
HIS FRIEND, ENCLOSING THE CONCLUDING
PORTION OF THE MANUSCRIPT.

Edinburgh, May 1818.

DEAR JOHN,

These three months I can find nothing to do. I am a burden on Jeanie and her husband. I wish I was a soldier again. I cannot even get labouring work. God will bless those, I hope, who have been good to me. I have seen my folly. I would be useful, but can get nothing to do. My mother is at her rest – God receive her soul! – I will go to South America. Maria de Parides will put me in a way to do for myself, and be a burden to no one. Or, I shall go to Spain, and live in Boho. – I will go to Buenos Ayres. – Farewell! John, this is all I have to leave you. It is yours: do with it as you think proper. If I succeed in the South, I will return and lay my bones beside my parents: if not, I will never come back.

THE END OF THE SOLDIERS JOURNAL

That closing letter may have been a device by John Howell to disguise the fact that 'Thomas' was really two different men; Joseph Sinclair and James Todd. Howell did refer to having used a journal which he obtained from his 'source'[10] and this would suggest that the journal was Sinclair's – he was an educated as well as observant lad – but if so it only covered the period from his enlistment up to his being sent to hospital after Fuentes d'Onoro. Why Howell then had to turn to Todd to finish the story may be explained by an entry in the parish register for Haddington in East Lothian. It was pointed out in a note to chapter one that Thomas' familiarity with the Bass and Tantallon Castle might indicate a connection with East Lothian and although there is no record of a Joseph Sinclair being born there – or in Edinburgh for that matter – a Joseph Sinclair from Edinburgh did marry Ann Edgar in Haddington on 24 August 1817. It is now impossible of course to positively determine whether he and the Joseph Sinclair who served in the 71st are one and the same, but they might be. At any rate, although his first name was recorded in error as Charles, Sinclair lived to claim his MGS with official bars for Rolieia, Vimeiro, Corunna, Vittoria, Pyrenees, Nive and Nivelle – and an unofficial one for Monte Video.[11]

Notes

Introduction

1 Essay by A.P. Woolrich in *Oxford Dictionary of National Biography*.

Chapter 1

1 As these events supposedly occurred in 1806 the writer must therefore have been born in 1790 and a search of the capital's parish registers reveals a James Todd was born there on 29 July 1790; the son of Alexander Todd and Janet Brown. This might be decisive were it not for the fact that, as will become apparent, the adventures related in this and the following chapter did not befall Todd.

2 Quintus Roscius Gallus, a Roman actor of some renown, defended by Cicero. 'Thomas' obviously had at least the rudiments of a classical education.

3 The first a substantial ruined castle on the shore and the second of course the Bass Rock; both prominent East Lothian landmarks. The Bass might have been a familiar name to anyone born and brought up in Edinburgh, but the author's familiarity with Tantallon suggests that he and his family originally came from East Lothian rather than the capital for both lie beyond North Berwick, some 20 miles to the east of Edinburgh.

4 A reference to the Limited Service Act 1806, introduced by William Windham. Instead of enlisting for life, recruits for the infantry could now engage for just seven years with an option to renew their engagement for a further two successive periods.

5 Establishing the equivalent value of money over 200 years ago is uncertain, particularly as the currency itself has completely changed. It is important, however, to understand how that currency worked; large sums were commonly expressed in guineas, of which more in a moment, but more mundane ones were expressed as pounds, shillings and pence, often rendered as £sd. There were 12 pennies to the shilling and 20 shillings to the pound. Until the withdrawal of gold coinage during the 1790s the pound was, however, an entirely notional concept and for actual transactions guinea pieces were preferred – gold coins each worth 21 shillings (or £1 1s).

6 While it is possible that this may simply have been a cant term for someone of a quiet and retiring disposition, the narrator of this portion of the narrative may indeed have been a Methodist; as this would certainly be consistent with his upbringing and would also explain why no trace of his baptism can be discovered in the Church of Scotland parish registers.

7 There was no soldier of this name serving in the 71st at this time. It is possible however that the man in question was a William Farquhar who went out to South America with 'Thomas'.

8 *WO12/7856-8.*

9 Illegitimate son of Earl of Tyrone, later Marquess of Waterford, born 2 October 1768. Early entries in *Army List* name him as Carr Beresford. Lost eye in shooting accident in Nova Scotia 1786. Served Toulon 1794. Took 88th Foot to India 1799 and served on Egyptian expedition under Baird 1801. Commanded brigade at capture of Cape 1806 and Buenos Aires expedition in same year. Taken prisoner but escaped after six months. Sent

to occupy Madeira late 1807. Served throughout Peninsular War. Assigned to reorganisation of Portuguese army with local rank of lieutenant general and Portuguese rank of marshal. Outstandingly successful administrator although his limited ability as field commander was demonstrated at Albuera 1811. Remained in Portugese service until 1819 revolution. Master general of ordnance 1828. Successively colonel 88th Foot 9 February 1807; 69th Foot 11 March 1819 and colonel 16th Foot 15 March 1823. Created viscount 1823; married cousin Louisa Beresford and died Bedgebury Park, Kent 8 January 1854, leaving no legitimate issue.

Commissions: ensign 16th Foot 27 August 1785; lieutenant 25 June 1789; captain Independent Company 24 January 1791; exchanged to 69th Foot 31 May 1791; major 1 March 1794; lieutenant colonel 124th Foot 11 August 1794; lieutenant colonel 88th Foot 1 September 1795; colonel (brevet) 1 January 1800; brigadier general 11 February 1804; major general (Portugal) 4 September 1807; major general 25 April 1808; lieutenant general 1 January 1812; general 27 May 1825.

Hall; *Hart(1840)*; *MGS*; *Oxford Dictionary of National Biography*.

10 *WO12/7856-8*. Thomas was attested on 25 July 1806 and the draft embarked on 11 August 1806.

11 Born New York 22 June 1758, second son of Dr Samuel Auchmuty, rector of Trinity Church, New York. Served North America; Brooklyn and White Plains. Served India 1783–1796, mainly in staff positions. Successively major of brigade and military secretary to Sir Robert Abercrombie, adjutant general. Returned to England 1797 and on leave of absence until 1800. Appointed to command 'corps' at Cape of Good Hope comprising 61st Foot, troop of cavalry and company of artillery – joined with Baird in attack on French – held Egypt by way of Suez. Commandant Isle of Thanet 1803. Brigadier 1806 – served South America. Returned to England

October 1807. Colonel 9th Garrison Battalion/103rd Foot 25 June 1808. CinC Madras 1810, commanded Java expedition August–September 1811. Colonel 78th Highlanders 13 January 1812. Returned to England 1813. CinC Ireland 1821. Dropped dead in Phoenix Park 11 August 1822.

Commissions: volunteer 45th Foot August 1776; ensign 45th 11 January 1777; lieutenant 15 August 1778, exchanged to 52nd Foot 21 February 1783; captain 75th Highlanders 8 November 1788; major (brevet) 30 April 1794; major 75th Highlanders 2 September 1795; lieutenant colonel (brevet) 22 September 1794; colonel (brevet) 5 January 1800; lieutenant colonel 58th Foot 25 September 1800; major general 25 April 1808; lieutenant general (Madras) 19 March 1810; lieutenant general 4 June 1813.

WO25/744; WO25/3998; Oxford Dictionary of National Biography.

12 Sir William Lumley 22nd Light Dragoons: seventh son of Richard Lumley 4th Earl of Scarborough and Barbara Savile, born 28 August 1769. Married (twice); died Grosvenor Square 15 December 1850. Served Ireland 1798, wounded in ankle during defence of Antrim 7 June 1798. Commanded 22nd Dragoons in Egypt 1801. Served South America, then Italy and Peninsula; commanded cavalry at Albuera. Invalided home August 1811. Governor of Bermuda 1819–1825. Colonel 6th Dragoons 3 November 1837.

Commissions: cornet 10th Light Dragoons 24 October 1787; lieutenant 19 May 1790; captain 4 December 1793; major Ward's Corps 10 March 1795; lieutenant colonel 22nd Light Dragoons 25 May 1795; colonel (brevet) 29 April 1802; major general 25 October 1809; lieutenant general 4 June 1814; general 10 January 1837.

Hart(1840); Oxford Dictionary of National Biography.

13 Colonel Gore Brown 40th Foot: served Helder 1799; Montevideo 1806; Walcheren 1809. Lieutenant governor of Plymouth 7 November 1812; colonel 6th Garrison Battalion

21 May 1813; colonel 44th Foot 29 January 1820. Died Weymouth 12 January 1843, aged 79.

Commissions: ensign 35th Foot 5 July 1780; lieutenant 3 March 1789; captain 83rd Foot 8 June 1793; major 15 June 1794; lieutenant colonel 7th West India Regiment 30 November 1796, exchanged to 40th Foot 5 August 1799; colonel (brevet) 1 January 1805; major general 25 July 1810; lieutenant general 12 August 1819; general 10 January 1837.

Gentlemans Magazine; *Hart(1840)*.

14 Probably Robert Campbell: served Cape; slightly wounded at Blauberg. Served South America, PoW Buenos Aires.

Commissions: ensign, 1st (Royal) Regiment 2 January 1779; lieutenant 1st (Royal) Regiment 13 October 1780; captain Independent Company 24 January 1791; half-pay 1791; major (brevet) 1 January 1798; captain 42nd Highlanders 9 July 1803; lieutenant colonel (brevet) 25 September 1803; captain half pay 108th Foot 22 September 1808; colonel (brevet) 1 January 1812; major general 4 June 1814.

WO25/3998; *Royal Military Calendar*.

15 Lieutenant General John Whitelocke: son of John White-locke, steward to Earl of Aylesbury, born 1757. Attended Lewis Lochee's military academy. Married/issue. Died 23 October 1833 at Beaconsfield, Bucks.

Served North America during revolutionary war as adjutant of Flank Battalion. Served Jamaica garrison 1782–1784 and again 1791–1793. Served St Domingo September 1793–June 1794 with local rank of colonel and acting as CinC until arrival of Brigadier General Whyte on 19 May. Then QMG but sent home with dispatches after capture of Port au Prince. Colonel 6th West India Regiment 1 September 1795. After further service in West Indies appointed brigadier general Guernsey 12 January 1798, lieutenant governor Portsmouth 29 May 1799. Commanded second Buenos Ayres expedition 1807. Court-martialled after surrender and cashiered 18 March 1808.

Commissions: ensign 14th Foot 14 December 1778; lieutenant 26 April 1780; captain 36th Foot 12 May 1784; major 60th Foot 2 October 1788; lieutenant colonel 13th Foot 30 March 1791; colonel (brevet) 21 August 1795; brigadier 10 September 1795; major general 18 June 1798; lieutenant general 2 November 1805.

16 Major General John Leveson Gower: son of Admiral John-Leveson Gower and Sarah Boscawen, born 25 June 1774. Second in command of La Plata expedition 1807. Married Isabella Mary Broke 27 December 1796/issue. Died 3 September 1816.

   Commissions: captain 9th Foot 16 January 1793; lieutenant colonel 63rd Foot 2 July 1794; colonel (late) 10th Garrison Battalion; major general 30 October 1805; lieutenant general 1 January 1812.

   Oxford Dictionary of National Biography.

17 Brigadier Gerneral Robert Craufurd – the celebrated 'Black Bob' Craufurd: third son of Sir Alexander Craufurd, born Newark, Ayrshire 5 May 1764. Served India 1790–1792. Resigned 17 October 1793 to undertake intelligence work on Continent, including liaison positions with Austrian Staff 1793–1797. Served Waldstein's Chasseurs and Hompesch's Chasseurs. DQMG Ireland 16 February 1798. Served as liaison officer with Russo-Austrian forces Switzerland 1799 and on Helder expedition same year. Adjutant general East Indies 17 September 1801. Commanded brigade at Buenos Aires, then commanded Light Brigade in Peninsula 1808; successfully evacuated it from Vigo. Returned to Peninsula with brigade 1809; subsequently enlarged to division. Fatally wounded at storming of Ciudad Rodrigo 19 January 1812 and died five days later.

   Commissions: ensign 25th Foot 1779; ensign 65th Foot 20 April 1780; ensign 26th Foot 28 April 1780; lieutenant 98th Foot 2 June 1780; lieutenant 26th Foot 7 March 1781; captain-lieutenant 45th Foot 19 March 1783; captain 92nd Foot

11 December 1782; captain 101st Foot 23 December 1783, on half-pay 1783 but exchanged to 75th Foot 1 November 1787; colonel (brevet) 26 January 1797; lieutenant colonel Hompesch, then 60th Foot 30 December 1797, lieutenant colonel 86th Foot 11 February 1802, half-pay 60th Foot 24 February 1803; colonel (brevet) 30 October 1805; brigadier general 16 September 1806; major general 4 June 1811.

WO25/3998; Hall; Oxford Dictionary of National Biography.

Chapter 2

1 This is not quite correct. The flanking force comprised Ferguson's Brigade (36th, 40th and 71st Regiments) and Bowes' Brigade (6th and 32nd Regiments). The attack in the centre was delivered by Hill's Brigade (5th, 9th and 38th Foot), Nightingale's Brigade (29th and 82nd Regiments), Crawford's Brigade (50th and 91st Regiments) and Fane's Brigade (45th, 5/60th and 2/95th Regiments).

2 The 29th's casualties accounted for nearly half of the total British loss, amounting to 190 officers and men, including six officers taken prisoner (Oman, Sir Charles, *History of the Peninsular War*, 1:240).

3 This comprised the 2/9th, 43rd, 52nd and 97th Regiments. The following day, another brigade (Acland's) was brought ashore, comprising the 2nd, 20th and 1/95th Regiments.

4 Ferguson's Brigade and the 82nd from Nightingale's Brigade were actually engaged at Ventosa about a mile and a half eastward of Vimiero, successfully fending off an attempt to turn Wellesley's left flank. The French commander, Solignac, was indeed captured along with just three guns.

5 Clark was wounded, but, anticipating Piper Findlater of the Fordons nearly a century later, sat up against a rock and continued to play his pipes as the regiment went into action

against a second French brigade commanded by General Brennier. Three more guns were taken in this charge. The 71st for their part lost 112 killed and wounded in the two fights. (Oman 1:259)

6 This was the Convention of Cintra, whereby in return for the surrender of Lisbon the French were permitted to evacuate Portugal and be carried home in British ships. Objectively it may have seemed a good settlement at the time, but the British generals concerned, Dalrymple, Burrard and Wellesley, were recalled to face a court of inquiry and only the latter escaped censure.

7 Sir John Moore, who took command of the British forces in Portugal on 6 October, was erroneously advised that the direct road from Lisbon to Salamanca was impractical for artillery and so sent his guns off by an unnecessarily circuitous route by way of Elvas with an escort comprising two cavalry regiments and four infantry battalions, including the 71st.

8 Son of John Hope, second Earl of Hoptoun, and his second wife, Jean Oliphant, born at Hopetoun House, Linlithgowshire, 17 August 1765. Married twice/issue. Died in Paris 22 August 1823.

Went to West Indies February 1795 but invalided home immediately on arrival, although subsequently did serve there under Abercromby until 1797. Subsequently at Helder 1799 and AAG to Abercromby in Mediterranean and Egypt – badly wounded, but recovered sufficiently to command brigade during final stages of campaign. Served Hanover 1805 and then Peninsula; succeeded to command of army after Moore killed and Baird badly wounded. Commanded reserve during Walcheren expedition 1809 and later appointed CinC Ireland in 1812, before returning to Peninsula 1813 to command 1st Division. Commanded left wing of army during invasion of France 1814, but wounded and PoW during sortie from Bayonne 14 April 1814.

Commissions: cornet 10th Light Dragoons 28 May 1784; lieutenant (late) 100th foot; lieutenant 27th Foot; captain 17th Light Dragoons 31 October 1789; major 1st (Royal) Regiment 1792; lieutenant colonel 25th Foot 26 April 1793; colonel (brevet) 3 May 1796; lieutenant general 25 April 1808.

Hall; Oxford Dictionary of National Biography.

9 Fifth son of William Baird, born at Newbyth House, Haddingtonshire 26 December 1757 and entered the Army in 1772. Served in India; wounded and captured at Polilur 10 September 1780 and held in chains at Sringapatnam until March 1794. Served on Mysore campaign 1791–1792 and at Pondicherry 1793. Led storming of Sringapatnam 1799 and commanded British and EIC contingent in Egypt 1801. On his return to India in 1802, he was employed against Sindhia, but being irritated at another appointment given to Wellesley he relinquished his command and returned to Europe. In 1804 he was knighted, and in 1805 commanded the expedition against the Cape of Good Hope, capturing Cape Town and forcing the Dutch general Janssens to surrender. On his return home he served in the Copenhagen expedition of 1807 where he was again wounded. Served Peninsula 1808–1809. Briefly commanded at Corunna before badly wounded in left arm – subsequently amputated. Knight Grand Cross of the Bath and a baronet in 1809. Colonel 2/54th Foot 9 May 1801; colonel 54th 8 May 1801; colonel 24th Foot 19 July 1807. Sir David married Miss Campbell-Preston, a Perthshire heiress, 4 August 1810. He was not employed again in the field, and personal and political enmities caused him to be neglected and repeatedly passed over although he did serve as CinC Ireland 1820–1822 before returning home following a riding accident. Appointed governor of Fort George but died at home Fernietower, Crieff, 18 August 1829.

Commissions: ensign 2nd Foot 16 December 1772; lieutenant 16 February 1778; captain (grenadier coy)

73rd/71st Highlanders 26 December 1778; major 5 June 1787; lieutenant colonel 8 December 1790; colonel (brevet) 21 August 1795; brigadier general (Cape) December 1797; major general 18 June 1798; lieutenant general 30 October 1805; general 4 June 1814.

WO25/3998; 1818 Pension Return; Hall; Oxford Dictionary of National Biography; Royal Military Calendar.

10 The same officer who took Buenos Aires.

11 The 71st commenced the campaign on 15 October 1808 764 strong and disembarked 626 in England in January, a loss of 138. (Oman 1:647)

12 Francis De Rottenburg: a Polish-born officer who entered the British Army in the mercenary Hompesch Hussars and was afterwards very influential in the development of light infantry tactics. His command experience, however, appears to have been less impressive.

Commissions: major Hompesch Hussars 25 December 1795; lieutenant colonel Hompesch Light Dragoons 25 January 1796; lieutenant colonel 60th Foot 30 December 1797; colonel (brevet) 1 January 1805; major general 25 July 1810.

WO25/748 R7.

13 'Sweet' Dennis Pack: only son of Very Reverend Thomas Pack, Dean of Ossory. Commanded 71st Highlanders at Buenos Aires, severely wounded and PoW but escaped and commanded provisional battalion until evacuation. Served Peninsula; in Portuguese service July 1810–April 1813, subsequently commanded brigade. Slightly wounded in Pyrenees 30 July 183 and badly wounded at Toulouse 10 April 1814. Served Waterloo – wounded. Colonel York Chasseurs 1815.

Married Lady Elizabeth Beresford 10 July 1816/issue. Died 24 July 1823.

Commissions: Cornet 14th Light Dragoons 30 November 1791; captain 5th Dragoon Guards 27 February 1796;

lieutenant colonel 71st Foot; colonel (brevet) 25 July 1810; major general 4 June 1813.

Dalton; Hall.

14 Bradburn Lees.

15 Not on the Military General Service medal roll.

Chapter 3

1 Seventh son of Charles 1st Earl of Cadogan, born 26 February 1780. Wounded at Buenos Aires; served Peninsula; initially as ADC to Wellington at Talavera, but then assumed command of 71st on their coming out; Fuentes d'Onoro, Alba de Tormes. Commanded brigade at Vittoria – killed in action there 21 June 1813.

Commissions: ensign 18th Foot 9 August 1797; lieutenant 18th Foot 18 July 1799; captain 60th Foot 21 November 1799; lieutenant and captain 2nd Footguards 9 December 1799; major 53rd Foot 8 December 1804; lieutenant colonel 18th Foot 22 August 1805; half-pay Brunswick Fencibles 5 March 1807; lieutenant colonel 71st Highlanders 7 January 1808; colonel (brevet) 4 June 1813.

WO25/2964; Hall; Oxford Dictionary of National Biography.

2 Part of Sir Brent Spencer's 1st Division.

3 Eldest son of General William Erskine of Torrie and Frances Moray. Served Peninsula; generally considered mad as well as incompetent. Committed suicide at Lisbon 13 February 1813.

Commissions: Second lieutenant 23rd Fusiliers 23 September 1785; lieutenant 13th Light Dragons 14 November 1787; captain 15th Light Dragoons 23 February 1791; major 15th Light Dragoons 1 March 1794; lieutenant colonel 15th Light Dragoons 14 December 1794, half-pay February

1796; colonel (brevet) 1 January 1801; colonel 14th Reserve Battalion 9 July 1803, half-pay February 1805; major general 25 April 1808.

WO25/3998; Hall.

4 Stopford's Brigade comprising 1/Coldstream and 1/Scots Guards.

5 Not Brunswickers but Kings German Legion (KGL) of Löw's Brigade.

6 Thomas was still serving with the 1st Division. The brigade, by then commanded by Kenneth Howard, was not transferred to 2nd Division until 6 June as part of the re-organisation which followed the battle of Albuera on 16 May.

7 Phillips Cameron: eldest son of Allan Cameron of Erracht who raised the 79th, born Knightsbridge 29 October 1782. Served Martinique 1796. Served Peninsula; fatally wounded at Fuentes d'Onoro 5 May 1811 and died 13 May.

Commissions: ensign 82nd Foot February 1794; lieutenant 91st Foot 26 March 1794; captain-lieutenant 79th Highlanders 6 June 1794; captain 79th Highlanders 8 October 1794; major 79th Highlanders 3 September 1801; lieutenant colonel 79th Highlanders 19 April 1804.

WO25/2965; Hall.

8 According to a return made on 1 May, two days before the battle, the 71st then had 42 officers and 455 men present and fit for duty. On 3 May casualties totalled one officer and seven men killed and five officers and thirty-three men wounded. On 5 May casualties were rather higher with two officers and eleven men killed and four officers and forty-seven wounded. A further two officers and thirty-seven men were returned as missing; presumably as prisoners. The total casualties, including prisoners, therefore amounted to 150 officers and men; rather than the 400 cited by Thomas, although the battalion was certainly the hardest hit in the brigade.

9   Again Thomas has a slightly hazy idea of the composition of the division: his own brigade as mentioned, comprised the 50th, 71st and 92nd, together with a company from 3/95th Rifles. Nightingall's Brigade comprised the 24th, 42nd and 79th, with a company from 5/60th Rifles. The KGL brigade under Löw had not one but four battalions, and of course Thomas omits to mention the Footguards.

10 Fought on 16 May 1811, the battle of Albuera saw an Anglo-Spanish Army commanded by generals Beresford and Blake out-generalled, out-flanked and comprehensively defeated by a French army under Marshal Soult. However, to the marshal's dismay neither of the allies refused to admit defeat and it was the French who retired in the end, but only after Beresford and Blake had lost some 6,000 killed and wounded out of 35,000; hence the battle's dubious sobriquet 'Bloody Albuera'. As a result of these losses, Howard's Brigade was transferred to the 2nd Division with effect from 6 June.

11 *WO12/7856.*

12 Sir Rowland, later Lord Hill: second son of Sir John Hill and Mary Chambre, born at Prees, Shropshire 11 August 1772 and studied at Strasbourg military academy. Created Baron Hill of Almaraz and Hardwicke 1814, viscount 1842. Died 10 December 1842 at Hardwick Grange.

Served as ADC to General O'Hara at Toulon. Served Egypt 1801. Commanded brigade on Hanover expedition. Served throughout Peninsular War, becoming Wellington's most trusted subordinate. Slightly wounded at Talavera. Commanded I Corps during Waterloo campaign (had horse shot under him) and served as 2nd Independent Company Army of Occupation 1815–1818. In retirement for next ten years, but made general 27 May 1825 and CinC Army 1828–1842. Colonel Royal Horse Guards 19 November 1830.

Commissions: ensign 38th Foot 31 July 1790; lieutenant 53rd Foot 24 January 1791; captain (brevet) 23 March 1793;

captain 86th Foot 30 October 1793; major 90th Foot 10 February 1794; lieutenant colonel 13 May 1794; colonel 1 January 1800; major general 30 October 1805; lieutenant general 1 January 1812; general 27 May 1825.

Dalton; Hall; Hart(1840); Oxford Dictionary of National Biography.

13 Two shillings and sixpence, or 25 pence in modern currency.

14 Possibly the William Caldwell who lived to claim the MGS with a bar for Toulouse.

Chapter 4

1 Served at Cape of Good Hope and Buenos Aires. Served throughout Peninsular War; slightly wounded at Vittoria 21 June 1813. Subsequently served in Ceylon. Died at Gloucester 24 January 1855, aged 68.

Commissions: ensign 71st Foot February 1800; lieutenant 16 July 1801; captain 71st Foot 25 March 1803; major 9 March 1809; lieutenant colonel (brevet) 19 June 1812; lieutenant colonel 71st Foot 13 October 1814; lieutenant colonel 2/83rd Foot 24 October 1816; half-pay 1818.

Gentlemans Magazine; Hall; Royal Military Calendar.

2 No return is available for the 71st, but the entire brigade, now commanded by Cadogan, mustered 120 officers and 2,657 rank and file at the outset of the campaign on 25 May 1813.

3 As usual an exaggeration, although the 71st did suffer higher casualties than anybody else in the brigade with three officers and forty-one men killed and twelve officers and 260 men wounded. One of them was Joseph Sinclair who was returned on the rolls as lying first in a field hospital at Vittoria itself and then in the general hospital at Bilbao. He would not return to the regiment for some months.

4 Some 40 men were taken prisoner when the four companies were ambushed (Oman 6:416).

5 Leslie Walker: served Peninsula; badly wounded at Sorauren. Served Waterloo.

Commissions: ensign 22 August 1799; lieutenant 23 August 1799; captain 28 August 1804; major, 71st Highlanders 2 September 1813; lieutenant colonel (brevet) 31 August 1815, exchanged to 25th Foot 1819; lieutenant colonel (unattached) 1 July 1828

Dalton; Hall.

6 Major Maxwell McKenzie: illegitimate son of John Mackenzie of Kincraig, Ross-shire. Served Peninsula; slightly wounded at Vimeiro 21 August 1808, badly wounded in Pyrenees 25 July 1813 and killed in action at the Nive 13 December 1813.

Commissions: ensign 87th Foot 28 October 1796; captain 71st Highlanders 25 June 1803; major (brevet) 30 May 1811; lieutenant colonel (brevet)

Hall; History of the Mackenzies.

7 The divisional commander Sir William Stewart: fourth son of John, 7th Earl of Galloway. Popularly known as 'Auld Grog Wullie'. Instrumental in forming Experimental Rifle Corps/95th Rifles; commanded same at Ferrol and Copenhagen. Colonel commandant 95th Rifles 31 August 1809. Served Peninsula; slightly wounded at Albuera, and badly wounded at Maya 25 July 1813, but remained strapped to saddle and in command of 2nd Division.

Commissions: ensign 42nd Highlanders March 1786; lieutenant 1787; captain independent company 24 June 1791; captain 22nd Foot 31 October 1792; major 31st Foot December 1794; lieutenant colonel (unattached) 14 January 1795; lieutenant colonel 67th Foot 1 September 1795; colonel (brevet) 1 January 1800; lieutenant colonel 95th Rifles 28 August 1800; major general 25 April 1808; colonel

3/95th Rifles 31 August 1809; lieutenant general 4 June 1813.
WO25/3998; Hall.

8   *WO12/7856.*

9   Sir Edward Barnes: commanded brigade at capture of Martinique and Guadaloupe. Served Peninsula; mainly on staff although commanded brigade in 7th Division at Vittoria, Pyrenees, Nivelle, Nive (wounded) and Orthes. Adjutant general at Waterloo – wounded. Afterwards served on staff in Ceylon and served as Governor 1824–1831. CinC India 1831–May 1833 with local rank of general. Colonel 2nd Garrison Battalion 27 November 1815; colonel 99th Foot 24 October 1816; colonel 78th Highlanders. Married Maria Fawkes 1824/issue. MP for Sudbury. Died in London 19 March 1838.

   Commissions: ensign 47th Foot 29 June 1793(?); lieutenant Independent Company 27 March 1793, exchanged to 86th Foot 30 October 1793; captain 99th Foot; major 16 November 1794, half-pay 1798; major 79th Highlanders 17 February 1800; lieutenant colonel (brevet) 1 January 1800; lieutenant colonel 46th Foot 23 April 1807; colonel (brevet) 25 July 1810; major general 4 June 1813.

   WO25/3998; Dalton; Hall; Oxford Dictionary of National Biography.

10   *Military History Society Bulletin 1* no.42:219 cites a statement by Howell that his source presented him with pages of a journal which he had kept.

11   Todd also lived to claim his MGS, with bars for Toleia, Vimeiro, Talavera, Fuentes d'Onoro, Vittoria, Pyrenees, Nivelle, Orthes and Toulouse. He also received the Waterloo medal.

Archival Sources

National Archives (Kew)

NA *WO12/7856* Regimental Muster Rolls 71st Foot

Other Contemporary Sources:

Cooper, Capt. T.H., *A Practical Guide for the Light Infantry Officer*, London, 1806

Rules and Regulations for the Formations, Field Exercise and Movements of His Majesty's Forces, 1792

Correspondence, Memoirs and Journals

Anton, James, *Retrospect of a Military Life*, Edinburgh, 1841

Howell, John (Ed.), *Journal of a Soldier of the 71st or Glasgow Regiment, Highland Light Infantry from 1806–1815*

Morris, Thomas, *Recollections*, London, 1845

Siborne, H.T., *Waterloo Letters: A Selection from Original and Hitherto Unpublished Letters Bearing on the Operations of the 16th, 17th, and 18th June, 1815, By Officers who served in the Campaign*, London, 1891

Wellington, 1st Duke of, *Dispatches of Field Marshal the Duke of Wellington*, ed. J. Gurwood, London, 1834–1838

—— *Supplementary Despatches and Memoranda of Field Marshal the Duke of Wellinton*, ed. 2nd Duke of Wellington, London, 1858–1872

Secondary Sources

Dalton, Charles, *The Waterloo Roll Call*, London, 1904

Fortescue, J.W., *History of the British Army*, London, 1899–1920

Garth, David Stewart of, *Sketches of the Character, Manners, and Present State of the Highlanders of Scotland, with Details of the Military Service of the Highland Regiments*, Edinburgh, 1822

Hall, Dr John A., *Biographical Dictionary of British Officers Killed and Wounded 1808–1814*, London, 1998

Haythornthwaite, Philip J., *The Napoleonic Source Book*, London, 1990

—— *The Armies of Wellington*, London, 1994

—— *Waterloo Men: The experience of Battle 16–18 June 1815*, Marlborough, 1999

Henderson, Diana, *Highland Soldier 1820–1920*, Edinburgh, 1989

Katcher, Philip, *King George's Army 1775–1783*, Reading, 1973

Lagden, A. and Sly, J.S., *The 2/73rd at Waterloo*, Brightlingsea, 1988 and 1998

Mullen, A.L.T., *The Military General Service Roll*, London, 1990

Oman, Sir Charles, *A History of the Peninsular War*, London, 1902–1930

Philippart, John, *Royal Military Calendar or Army Service and Commission Book*, London, 1820

Reid, Stuart, *Wellington's Officers: Biographical Dictionary of the Field Officers and Staff Officers of the British Army 1793–1815, Vol.1 A–G*, Southend, 2008

—— *Wellington's Highlanders*, London, 1992

—— *British Redcoat (1)*, Oxford, 1996

—— *British Redcoat (2)*, Oxford, 1997

—— *Redcoat Officer*, Oxford, 2002

—— *Wellington's Army in the Peninsula*, Oxford, 2004

INDEX

Other books on the Napoleonic Wars published by
Frontline Books include:

1809 THUNDER ON THE DANUBE
Napoleon's Defeat of the Habsburgs
John H Gill
Volume I: Abensberg ISBN 978-1-84415-713-6
Volume II: Aspern ISBN 978-1-84832-510-4
Volume III: Wagram and Znaim ISBN 978-1-84832-547-0

ALBUERA 1811
The Bloodiest Battle of the Peninsular War
Guy Dempsey
Foreword by Donald E. Graves
ISBN 978-1-84832-499-2

DRAGON RAMPANT
The Royal Welch Fusiliers at War, 1793–1815
Donald E. Graves
ISBN 978-1-84832-551-7

NAPOLEON'S INVASION OF RUSSIA
Theodore Ayrault Dodge
Foreword by George F. Nafziger
ISBN 978-1-84832-501-2

THE WATERLOO ARCHIVE
Edited by Gareth Glover
Volume I: British Sources ISBN 978-1-84832-540-1
Volume II: German Sources ISBN 978-1-84832-541-8

A WATERLOO HERO
The Reminiscences of Friedrich Lindau
Friedrich Lindau
Edited and Presented by James Bogle and Andrew
Uffindel
ISBN 978-1-84832-539-5

WELLINGTON'S HIGHLAND WARRIORS
From the Black Watch Mutiny to the Battle of Waterloo
Stuart Reid
Foreword by Philip Haythornthwaite
ISBN 978-1-84832-557-9

For more information on our other books, please visit
www.frontline-books.com. You can write to us at
info@frontline-books.com or at
47 Church Street, Barnsley, S. Yorkshire, S70 2AS.